FUNDAMENTALS OF SMALL BUSINESS MANAGEMENT

Dr. V. RAMANUJAM

Dr S PAVITHRA

Contents

Preface

This book delvers into the key principles, strategies, and challenges associated with entrepreneurship and small business management, offering insights into their essential roles in shaping the future of business and society. Entrepreneurship is the process of starting, managing, and scaling a business. It combines innovation, skills, and vision to create new products, services, or ideas that meet market demand and create value for a target audience. Entrepreneurs are individuals or small groups of partners who take on the most risk associated with a business venture. In addition, they stand to gain the most from the project's success.

Entrepreneurship and small business management serve as the cornerstones of innovation, economic growth, and societal development. This material is designed to guide aspiring entrepreneurs, business enthusiasts, and management professionals on a comprehensive journey through the dynamics of starting, managing, and scaling a business.

PREFACE

The content encapsulates key concepts of entrepreneurship, various types of entrepreneurial ventures, critical management practices for small businesses, and strategic tools to navigate today's competitive markets. From understanding entrepreneurial mindsets and competencies to mastering the nuances of feasibility studies, business planning, and organizational management, this material serves as both a learning resource and a practical manual.

Recognizing the transformative role of small businesses in shaping communities and economies, this work integrates real-world examples, actionable strategies, and step-by-step frameworks. It emphasizes the balance between innovative thinking and systematic management, ensuring that learners are equipped with the skills to address challenges and seize opportunities. We hope this material empowers readers to pursue their entrepreneurial dreams, foster sustainable growth, and contribute meaningfully to the evolving business landscape.

Dr. V. RAMANUJAM

Dr S PAVITHRA

SMALL BUSINESS MANAGEMENT

(For BBA/B.Com./M.B.A./M.Com. or Supportive/Value added/Job oriented paper for any under graduation/post-graduation programme)

Course Outcome: To teach how to plan for success, market products or services, find the right sources to finance a business, and write an effective business plan step-by-step to start your own small business or manage a small business for someone else.

Course Objectives:

- Identify the typical qualities and behaviours of successful entrepreneurs, and the benefits and drawbacks of starting one's own business, buying a franchise, and purchasing an existing business.
- Identify an appropriate business structure to match the business plan, including factors, proceedings, issues and feasibility report of small business.
- Identify the components of a solid business team such as employees, suppliers, and distributors, and techniques used in identifying personal and business characteristics that will enhance a business.
- Recognize the features and benefits of different types of funding in order to identify the right money sources for a particular business and identify the risk involved in small business management and ethics in small business.

Unit 1: Entrepreneurship and Small Business: Introduction, Definition-Role & Importance-Types of Entrepreneurship & Examples-Required Skills and Competencies of Entrepreneur-Small Business in India: Definition, impact and importance.

Unit 2: Starting a Small Business (Business plan and feasibility): Steps and Aspects for starting a new business- starting a business: Factors and proceedings & Issues-Feasibility report for small business-Business Plan: How to Develop a Feasibility Plan

Unit 3: Small Business: Marketing and HR management: Definition-Functions-Competitive advantage- Sales-Strategies for Business Growth-Marketing Strategy Types: **Human Resource Management:** Definitions-Objectives-Responsibilities- Managing HR in Small Business Management

Unit 4: Financing and Budgeting in Small Business: Financial Planning process- Start up budget - overview and cost- Funding Opportunities for SBM: Bootstrapping- Angel Investors- Short Term Financing- Crowd Funding

Unit 5: **Risk Management in Small Business:** External Environmental Change drive the need for Risk Management- Ways to Manage Risk: insurable and uninsurable- **Ethics in Small Business**: Theories and principles- Ethical Decision making: process-steps and principles- social responsibility in organisation.

CHAPTER - 1 Fundamentals of Entrepreneurship

1.1 Introduction
1.2 Entrepreneurship and Small Business Management
1.3 Different Types of Entrepreneurships with Examples
1.4 Key Competencies needed to become an entrepreneur
1.5 How to Develop Entrepreneurial Abilities?
1.6 Chapter Summary
1.7 Multiple choice questions
1.8 Short type questions
1.9 Essay type questions
1.10 Mini- Case Study
1.11 References

1.1 INTRODUCTION

Students who want to start their own enterprises or work in small businesses that are focused on growth can have a unique learning experience with the Entrepreneurship and Small Business Management course. Every business is built on entrepreneurship. Every major corporation was once a tiny enterprise run by an entrepreneur. Possessing the abilities and know-how to launch a new company could be the difference between wealth and poverty as our economy grows more unstable.

Established businesses also need people with entrepreneurial qualities. To thrive, any business, regardless of size, needs to possess an entrepreneurial spirit. The company's motto of "do it our way" has been substituted with creative thinking.

1.2 ENTREPRENEURSHIP AND SMALL BUSINESS MANAGEMENT:

The fields of entrepreneurship and small business management are linked, promoting innovation, economic growth, and business landscape shaping. Even though they are closely connected, they each have unique components of the entrepreneurial journey, from the beginning of new projects to managing the daily operations of already-existing companies. Entrepreneurship embodies the spirit of creativity, risk-taking, and vision as individuals identify opportunities, innovate solutions, and transform ideas into viable enterprises. Small business management, on the other hand, is concentrated on the effective use of resources, strong leadership, and strategic decision-making required for enterprises to expand and survive in a cutthroat marketplace. An active and dynamic entrepreneurial environment is formed by small business management and entrepreneurship. With the help of this system, people can follow their dreams of becoming entrepreneurs and improve communities and economies all across the world.

1.3 DIFFERENT TYPES OF ENTREPRENEURSHIPS WITH EXAMPLES

Taking the risk to develop something new and exercising initiative have always been key components of entrepreneurship. These days, innovation can take many various shapes. This is our guide to 12 different kinds of entrepreneurship, each of which highlights the unique qualities of an entrepreneur.

a) **Traditional Entrepreneurship:** The most prevalent type of entrepreneurship is this one. It emphasizes on launching and operating a company with profit as the main objective. These companies usually offer products or services in return for cash, and profitability, market share, and revenue are used to gauge a business's performance. **Example:** A local bakery is a classic example of traditional entrepreneurship, often driven by a passionate baker with a cherished family recipe. These business owners are motivated to start their endeavors by the community's need for superior baked goods. Success in this field relies on several key factors, including the quality and taste of their products, their dedication to providing exceptional customer service, and their ability to cultivate a loyal customer base. Customers are drawn to the convenience and homely charm of a neighbourhood bakery. "There are a ton of additional instances of conventional entrepreneurship. These consist of local retail establishments, manufacturing, consulting firms, clothing boutiques, and service-oriented companies.

a) Social Entrepreneurship: The goal of social entrepreneurs is to create income while simultaneously addressing environmental or social issues. They put society effect ahead of maximizing profits. Goonj is a prime illustration of social entrepreneurship. It is a social enterprise whose mission is to collect abandoned apparel from cities. They donate these things to persons in need in the area after sorting and fixing them. Another illustration is Grameen Bank, which promotes entrepreneurship and economic development in Bangladesh and abroad by providing microloans to the disadvantaged, mostly women. Here are some social entrepreneurship ideas:

Table 1.1: Entrepreneurial Ideas of Social Enterprises

Sector	**Nature of Business**
Education Access	Online learning platform for underserved communities, School building projects in developing countries.
Healthcare Services	Mobile healthcare clinics, Affordable medicine distribution
Empowerment of Marginalized Groups	Women's cooperative for artisanal crafts, Youth empowerment programs
Environmental Conservation	Reforestation projects, Plastic waste recycling social enterprise
Tech for Good	Tech solutions for social issues, Digital literacy and skills training
Fair Trade and Ethical Supply Chains	Fair trade coffee cooperative, Ethical fashion label supporting artisans

Renewable Energy Access	Solar energy microgrid projects, Biogas digester installations
Community Development and Empowerment	Community-owned social enterprises, Skills development and vocational training centers

b) Serial Entrepreneurship: Serial entrepreneurs aren't content with just one business idea. They are motivated by the challenge of creating something effective from the ground up and a never-ending supply of fresh ideas. Serial entrepreneurs normally concentrate on one firm at a time, seeing it through to a certain point before moving on to the next, while some may manage several projects at once. Attaining profitability, securing a particular market share, or even selling the company outright are examples of this stage. The Hustlers are another name for these business owners. One well-known example is Elon Musk, who founded businesses including PayPal, SpaceX, and Tesla. Renowned Indian serial entrepreneur Krishnan Ganesh is well-known for his profitable businesses, which include Big Basket, Bluestone, TutorVista, and more.

c) Corporate Entrepreneurship:

Intrapreneurship, another name for corporate entrepreneurship, upends the conventional paradigm. Rather than individuals striking out on their own, it's about staff members acting like entrepreneurs within a well-established company. Within their current organization, intrapreneurs seek for and create new initiatives or projects. They contribute a new viewpoint and a willingness to take measured chances in order to spur innovation and expansion for the larger company. One example of a corporate entrepreneur is Peri Hartman, an internal coder at Amazon. One of the main contributing factors to Amazon's rise was the breakthrough 'purchase with one-click' technology that he invented. One more instance is the finding of sticky notes. In an attempt to produce a very sticky glue, 3M scientist Dr. Spencer Silver produced a somewhat sticky material.

d) Imitative Entrepreneurship: This is the practice of copying an established product, service, or business model into a new market or environment. Imitative entrepreneurs find profitable business concepts, goods, or services that have worked well elsewhere and modify them to fit their needs rather than coming up with something completely original. Even if it might take more creativity and originality to create something completely new, imitative entrepreneurship can still be a successful tactic, particularly in markets where there is a need for tried-and-true goods or services. For imitation entrepreneurs to successfully copy current models and fight successfully in the markets they target, they must possess strong execution, adaption, and market research skills. For instance, Ola began as a ride-hailing competitor of Uber, copying its business strategy while focusing on the Indian market. Ola made adjustments, such as adding traditional taxis to its line-up in addition to services like auto-rickshaws and bike taxis, which are popular forms of transportation in India. Flipkart, also called the "Amazon of India," is another example. It first copied Amazon's e-commerce strategy but then modified its offerings to better meet the needs and tastes of the Indian market. Because credit card usage is so low in India, the company created features like cash on delivery and personalized its offerings to suit a wide range of regional preferences.

e) Tech Entrepreneurship: This fascinating field involves creating companies centered on cutting-edge technological goods or services. These business owners employ technology to solve issues, open up new markets, and upend long-standing sectors of the economy. These businesspeople don't hesitate to question the existing quo and create innovative solutions that stretch the bounds of what's conceivable. Product development, software development, hardware development, data management, cybersecurity, user experience design, cloud computing, internet of things, block chain technology, networking and infrastructure, quality assurance, testing, and other technical aspects are all essential to the success of tech entrepreneurship. An iconic example is Microsoft, which was created by Paul Allen and Bill Gates. Microsoft was a major player in the personal computing revolution with its Windows operating system and Office productivity suite. Amazon was created by Jeff Bezos and swiftly grew to become one of the biggest e-commerce businesses globally.

f) Green Entrepreneurship: Green entrepreneur creates goods and services that are sustainable for the environment, encouraging eco-friendly behavior and lowering carbon footprints. Urban farming and agritech, sustainable fashion firms, zero-waste lifestyle enterprises, green building and construction, renewable energy companies, and environmental consulting and services are a few instances of green entrepreneurship. For instance, YashPakka Vice Chairman Ved Krishna is a visionary businessman committed to the global abolition of single-use plastics. Ved is the company's leader in producing biodegradable tableware and packaging paper from sugarcane waste. Profit and sustainability are now aligned, which have won YashPakka significant accolades like the India Design Mark and Red Dot. The founder of Bambrew, Vaibhav Anant, is driving a sustainable packaging firm that is transforming the Indian market. By providing natural alternatives, Bambrew has successfully eliminated over 10,000 tons of plastic garbage under his direction. Vaibhav is changing the market landscape with his vision of sustainable alternatives through strategic alliances with large brands like Amazon and Puma. These are some ideas for green business initiatives that one can start on their own.

Table No. 1.2 - Examples of Green Entrepreneurship

Sector	**Nature of Business**
Eco-Friendly Transportation	**Electric Vehicle (EV) Charging Stations:** Establish charging stations for electric cars in urban areas. Initiate a program that provides short-distance bicycle rentals for those who commute by bicycle.
Sustainable Agriculture	**Urban Farming:** Utilize empty urban spaces to cultivate organic fruits and vegetables. **Aquaponics Farming:** Establish an aquaponics farm by fusing hydroponics—the process of growing plants in water—with aquaculture, the practice of rearing fish.
Green Construction	**Green Building Materials:** Green Building Produce and market environmentally friendly building supplies, such as bamboo, repurposed wood, or concrete with minimal emissions. **Energy-Efficient Home Retrofitting:** Offer services to upgrade existing homes with energy-saving features like insulation, LED lighting, and efficient appliances.
Environmental Consulting	**Sustainability Auditing:** Provide evaluations to companies about their environmental impact and offer suggestions for enhancements through environmental consulting and sustainability auditing. **Carbon Footprint Reduction Strategies:** Provide advisory services to assist businesses in cutting

	their carbon footprints and becoming more environmentally friendly.
Ethical Fashion	**Sustainable Clothing Line:** Establish an online marketplace where people may purchase and sell gently used apparel and accessories. **Second-hand Fashion Marketplace:** Create an online platform for buying and selling pre-owned clothing and accessories.
Eco-Tourism	**Nature-Based Tours:** Plan environmentally responsible tours that raise awareness of environmental issues and wildlife conservation. Eco-Lodges: Construct lodging in unspoiled areas with an emphasis on sustainability and a low environmental footprint.

g) International Entrepreneurship: This entails operating a business internationally, reaching out to a variety of markets, and customizing goods and services to fit various regulatory, cultural, and economic contexts. These endeavours frequently call for a thorough comprehension of international trade dynamics and worldwide markets. For instance, Apple started off selling computers locally. They opened their first store in Tokyo, Japan, as part of a calculated international expansion strategy after being well-established in the US market. Understanding the worldwide market while adhering to its brand identity of revolutionary design and user-friendliness was the key to Apple's success.

h) Scalable Start-up Entrepreneurship: These businesses aim to become giants of their field and see rapid growth in a short amount of time. They spot big holes in big markets and fill them with creative fixes, be it a ground-breaking tech product, a game-changing company plan, or an entirely new method of operating. Scalable start-ups frequently look to venture investors seeking high-risk, high-reward prospects for sizable investments. With the help of this infusion of capital, they are able to quickly grow their business by launching forceful marketing campaigns, erecting a sturdy infrastructure, or hiring top talent. These firms want to become household names in their industry by utilizing high-growth techniques and taking advantage of the surge in customer demand. For instance, Airbnb's website offers distinctive lodging options and genuine travel experiences as an alternative to conventional hotels. Airbnb quickly grew its global footprint and revolutionized travel and destination experiences by leveraging the sharing economy and user-generated content. Ola upended the taxi industry by providing millions of users with dependable, reasonably priced, and convenient transportation options. Thanks to its scalable business strategy, the company was able to quickly grow into other markets, broaden its offerings, and provide things like out-of-town travel, luxury rides, and auto rentals.

i) Small Business Entrepreneurship: Small business entrepreneurship is a vital component of local economies and the backbone of many communities. These company owners create and run tiny enterprises, frequently catering to a niche clientele in a particular region. Small business owners are well-versed in the demands and preferences of their clientele and have a keen awareness of the community in which they operate. As an illustration: Pet sitting and dog walking, online tuition, handmade crafts, food trucks, freelance writing, coaching, etc. are a few examples of small businesses. Event planning, social media management, Homemade baked goods, Virtual assistant, Graphic design services, home renovation services, Personal chef services, Gardening and landscaping, Language translation services, Mobile repair services, E-commerce store, etc.

j) Non-Profit Entrepreneurship: For people who are motivated to have a beneficial social or environmental impact, non-profit entrepreneurship is a potent career route. It entails founding organizations that deal with important problems, but unlike traditional businesses, making money isn't the main objective. Non-profit entrepreneurship encompasses groups such as charities, NGOs, and community development organizations. An example of a typical non-profit organization that encourages innovation in governance and social enterprises, increases young participation in development, and improves access to education is the Dr. A.P.J. Abdul Kalam Centre, which was founded by Srijan Pal Singh.

k) Franchise Entrepreneurship: Aspiring company owners have a distinct route to go with franchise entrepreneurship. Franchise owners buy the rights to use a franchisor's brand name to run a certain business model. This implies that one will manage on their own franchise location while taking advantage of the franchisor's well-established brand, clever marketing plans, and operational know-how. Examples: Arguably the most famous example of franchise entrepreneurship, McDonald's has a global presence with thousands of franchise locations worldwide. Franchisees gain from the company's well-known brand, established procedures, and comprehensive training. One of the biggest franchise businesses in the world, Subway prides itself on using only the freshest ingredients and creating sandwiches that can be customized. Franchisees benefit from the freedom to customize their menu to suit regional preferences while taking use of Subway's supply chain and marketing assistance.

1.4 Key Competencies Needed to Become an Entrepreneur:

a. **Proficiency in Business Management:** For entrepreneurs to effectively plan, organize, direct, and control an organization's resources, they must possess business management abilities. These abilities can increase a company's credibility, boost productivity, control risks, put successful plans into action, foster a pleasant workplace culture, and expand its clientele. Business management skills include:

- Leadership
- Strategic thinking
- Budget management
- Business acumen
- Communication

b. Communication and Listening: People with good communication skills can write, speak, and express themselves in a clear and concise manner using a variety of media. The capacity to comprehend, retain, and react correctly to information is a function of listening skills. Important entrepreneurship skills include effective communication and listening in order to build relationships, resolve conflicts, understand requirements and perspectives, and make well-informed decisions. Communication and listening skills include:

- Written communication
- Non-verbal communication
- Stress management
- Active listening
- Emotion control

c. Critical and Creative Thinking Skills: To establish and grow their companies, entrepreneurs need to possess strong critical and creative thinking abilities. By applying critical thinking, you can make well-informed decisions and find solutions to issues by objectively analysing information and the supporting data. Thinking creatively gives one the ability to see problems from several viewpoints, consider other approaches, and generate unique ideas. Critical and creative thinking skills include:

- Analysis

- Brainstorming
- Visualization
- Evaluation
- Research

d. **Strategic Thinking and Planning Skills:** These abilities enable business owners to analyse data, adjust, oversee initiatives, resolve issues, and reach well-informed conclusions. These entrepreneurial abilities are essential for assisting leaders in overcoming obstacles, ensuring effective resource allocation, and achieving objectives. Strategic thinking and planning skills include:

- Analysis
- Implementation
- Flexibility
- Attention to detail
- Assertiveness

e. **Branding, Marketing, and Networking Skills:** These three areas are crucial for expanding the company and creating possibilities in the cutthroat business world of today. Entrepreneurs can market and sell goods and services with these abilities. While branding creates a unique and lasting image of a product, service, or organization, marketing simply gets the word out to the target market. People can communicate and build relationships with potential partners, suppliers, customers, and co-workers through networking. Branding, marketing, and networking skills include:

- Collaboration
- Communication
- Interpersonal skills
- Creativity
- Collaboration

e. **Entrepreneurial Skills in the Workplace:** These are the abilities that people need to successfully launch and run their own companies, as well as spur innovation and expansion inside larger institutions. Entrepreneurial skills in the workplace include:

- Time management
- Finance skills
- Sales
- Adaptability
- Problem-solving

f. **Teamwork and Leadership Abilities:** These are two extremely important entrepreneurship abilities that promote a cooperative and happy work environment, which boosts productivity and employee happiness. These attributes can help leaders work in teams, inspire and encourage others, and steer the business in the direction of success. Teamwork and leadership skills include:

- Communication
- Emotional intelligence
- Empathy
- Delegation
- Conflict resolution

g. **Time Management and Organizational Skills:** Effective leaders understand how to assign and prioritize work, control their own time and resources, and keep their workspace organized and productive. Possessing good time management and organizing abilities can help you accomplish objectives, control stress, preserve a positive work-life balance, and enhance happiness and wellbeing. Time management and organizational skills include:

- Multi-tasking
- Decision making
- Collaboration

h. **Sales Skills:** Since entrepreneurs must be able to pitch their companies to investors and possible clients, sales skills are important for both salespeople and business owners. Gaining confidence in sales can help business owners close deals, present their ideas to potential investors, engage in productive negotiations, and forge strong bonds with stakeholders, clients, and investors. Sales skills include:

- Business acumen
- Negotiation
- Relationship-building
- Data analysis
- Social selling

i. **Stress Management Skills:** An entrepreneur's health may suffer as a result of running a company. For the benefit of themselves, their staff, and their company, they must be able to effectively handle and cope with stress. Leaders that possess stress management abilities can improve their general quality of life, preserve good physical and mental health, and strengthen their personal and professional connections. Stress-reduction techniques include: mindfulness, meditation, positive thinking, sleep hygiene, and exercise.

1.5 How to Develop Entrepreneurial Abilities?

One can hone their entrepreneurial abilities in the following ways:

- **Specify objectives:** List the company's aims, advantages, disadvantages, and desired outcomes.
- **Learn:** Books, seminars, and podcasts can all be excellent resources for knowledge to improve your abilities.
- **Enrol in online classes:** Taking classes online is a great method to improve the skills.
- **Seek for a mentor:** Seeking mentorship from outstanding leaders can significantly impact the life and career of a person.
- **Put in a lot of work:** Establish a solid work ethic and be persistent in the endeavours to advance.
- **Stay Adaptive:** Encourage a growth mentality by being flexible and willing to accept new possibilities and ideas as they present themselves.
- **Develop a positive mind-set:** Put an emphasis on lifelong learning and look for fresh chances to advance in the career.

1.6 Chapter Summary

Entrepreneurship has a significant role in the expansion of the national economy. Therefore, it's critical to recognize the driving forces behind entrepreneurship and provide an explanation for why some people succeed in this endeavour more than others. A business is supported by the community. It is therefore a segment of society, as we would say. In the social setting, they have a strong relationship in which they influence one another and split the profits and losses. Maintaining a healthy balance is important in this interplay between affecting and being impacted. The goal of the practice of entrepreneurship development is to increase people's capacity for entrepreneurship. Put another way, it's the development, refinement, and instillation of entrepreneurial traits that a person needs in order to launch and effectively manage a business. Through entrepreneurship development, people can acquire the motivation and business acumen needed to launch and grow a profitable company. It all comes down to creating fresh ideas and developing those ideas into a successful business from the ground up.

1.7 Multiple Choice Questions

1. An individual who undertakes the creation, organization and ownership of a business is called (an):
    - A) Investor
    - B) Business broker
    - C) Role model
    - D) Entrepreneur

    Answer: (D)

2. Selling and shipping products to another country is called:
    - A) Importing
    - B) Trade barriers
    - C) Exporting
    - D) Trade Missions

    Answer: (C)

1.8 Short Type Questions

1. What do you understand by 'entrepreneurship'?
2. What are the characteristics of successful entrepreneur?
3. How to develop entrepreneurial abilities?

1.9 Essay Type Questions

1. Describe the various types of entrepreneurships in India. Explain with suitable example of each.
2. Explain the importance and need for small business in Indian economy in the modern era.
3. Discuss the key competencies needed to become an entrepreneur

1.10 Mini- Case Study:

A young entrepreneur launches an innovative mobile app for local food delivery. The entrepreneur navigates challenges such as identifying a market gap, securing initial customers, and developing a unique value proposition. The study will analyse how the fundamentals of entrepreneurship such as opportunity recognition, risk-taking, and innovation play a role in the business's success.

Questions:

- What were the key entrepreneurial challenges the business owner faced when launching the mobile app?
- How did the entrepreneur identify the market gap, and how did that influence the success of the app?
- What strategies did the entrepreneur use to mitigate risks and ensure innovation?

1.11 References

1. Barringer, B. R., & Ireland, R. D. (2020). *Entrepreneurship: Successfully launching new ventures* (6th ed.). Pearson.
2. Longenecker, J. G., Petty, J. W., Palich, L. E., & Hoy, F. (2019). *Small business management: Launching and growing entrepreneurial ventures* (19th ed.). Cengage Learning.
3. Kuratko, D. F. (2021). *Entrepreneurship: Theory, process, practice* (11th ed.). Cengage Learning.
4. https://www.proprofs.com/quiz-school/story.php?title=going-into-business-yourself-sep-28-2009

Chapter -2: Basics of Small Business Management

2.1 Introduction

Small business management encompasses the alignment and coordination of all facets of a small firm, including hiring staff, managing suppliers, overseeing money, creating a plan, and carrying out daily activities. Running a small business is challenging, particularly in light of the constant changes in consumer demands, technological advancements, and marketing tactics. What are some strategies for managing a start-up firm that ensures smooth scaling up when the time comes, all the while keeping an eye on the future? You probably handle a variety of various departments inside the company, so you have a lot on one's plate and have to wear several hats.

Using real-world start up and small business examples that are prospering and preparing for growth, this article explains how to run small businesses correctly. Aligning and coordinating every facet of a small organization is part of small business management. This can involve overseeing all day-to-day operations of the company as well as personnel, vendors, and finances. The big-picture business strategy will frequently be under the management of a small business manager.

2.2 Small Business Management: What Is It?

Aligning and managing every facet of a small organization is the responsibility of small business management. This entails managing the company's everyday operations as well as its staff, vendors, and money. A small business manager is frequently also responsible for managing the overall business plan. Among the many duties of this position are the following:

- Hiring, orienting, and training staff
- Handling financial issues
- Building the company's reputation in the marketplace
- Managing the channels of distribution and inventories
- Establishing corporate objectives and strategic aims
- Ensuring client contentment
- Outlining a clear business strategy
- Examining corporate data to make well-informed decisions

It's a complex role that needs smart management and strong leadership to make sure the company succeeds and lasts.

2.3 Entrepreneurship and Small Business Management

In order to propel corporate success and economic growth, entrepreneurship and small business management are tightly related. This is how they enhance one another:

a) **Idea Generation and Venture Creation:** By producing creative ideas and spotting market openings, entrepreneurship stimulates the development of new businesses. Small business management offers the framework and procedures required to successfully manage and expand the enterprise once it has been founded.

b) **Strategic Planning and Execution**: Creating business plans and strategic visions to direct the venture's expansion and growth is a key component of entrepreneurship. Small business management ensures effective execution and alignment with business objectives by translating these plans into doable actions.

c) **Allocation of Resources and Financial Management:** To start their businesses, entrepreneurs frequently obtain the initial capital and resources. In order to maintain and expand the company over time, small business management focuses on maximizing profitability, managing money, and allocating resources as efficiently as possible.

d) **Operational Efficiency and Process Improvement:** To increase operational efficiency and competitiveness, entrepreneurship fosters innovation and process improvement. Systems and procedures are put in place by small business management to control workflows, increase productivity, and streamline operations.

e) **Risk Management and Adaptability:** Being an entrepreneur means having to manage risk and adjust to shifting market conditions. Effective navigation of uncertainties and obstacles through flexibility, contingency planning, and risk reduction measures are the main themes of small business management.

f) **Resource Allocation and Financial Management:** Entrepreneurs usually raise the first funding and resources needed to launch their companies. Small business management is focused on optimizing profitability, handling finances, and allocating resources as effectively as possible in order to sustain and grow the company over time.

g) **Operational Efficiency and Process Improvement:** Innovation and process improvement are encouraged by entrepreneurship in order to boost operational efficiency and competitiveness. Small business management implements processes and procedures to optimize operations, boost productivity, and regulate workflows.

h) **Risk Management and Adaptability:** Managing risk and making adjustments to changing market conditions are essential components of becoming an entrepreneur. The key components of small business management include flexibility, backup plans, and risk mitigation strategies for successfully navigating uncertainties and roadblocks.

The structure, procedures, and managerial skills needed to support and expand new businesses over time are provided by small business management, whereas entrepreneurship offers the vision, inventiveness, and drive to launch new ones. They have a mutually beneficial relationship that promotes economic growth, corporate success, and societal impact.

2.4 Benefits of Entrepreneurship and Small Business Management

The following are some salient features of small business management and entrepreneurship:

a) **Innovation and Creativity:** Finding opportunities and coming up with creative solutions to take advantage of them are key components of entrepreneurship. Innovation in product creation, marketing tactics, and business operations is fostered by small business management.

b) **Risk-taking and Resilience:** In order to develop company ideas, entrepreneurs frequently take calculated risks. Resilience is necessary for small business management to overcome obstacles and failures encountered along the route.

c) **Flexibility and Adaptability:** Successful small business owners and entrepreneurs need to be able to adjust to shifting consumer tastes, market conditions, and levels of competition.

d) **Customer Focus:** Understanding client demands and providing value through goods and services are critical components of both small business management and entrepreneurship.

e) **Financial Management:** Small firms must practice effective financial management if they want to survive. Small business owners and entrepreneurs need to manage their cash flow, create a budget, and look for capital when needed.

f) **Networking and Collaboration:** For entrepreneurs and small company owners, establishing a network of connections and working together with others can be a great way to get chances, resources, and support.

g) **Goal-Setting and Planning:** Managers of small businesses and entrepreneurs create strategic plans and set measurable objectives. This include setting goals, laying out a plan of action, and tracking advancement toward achievement.

h) **Ethics and Social Responsibility:** Upholding moral principles and acting responsibly is crucial to preserving the confidence of clients, staff members, and the community. Social and environmental concerns are frequently incorporated into business operations by entrepreneurs and small business managers.

2.5 Distinctions Between Small Business Management and Entrepreneurship:

This table highlights the main differences and emphasizes the special traits and areas of emphasis between small business management and entrepreneurship.

Table 2.1 - Difference Between Entrepreneurship and Small Business Management

Aspect	Entrepreneurship	Small Business Management
Focus	Creation of new ventures, novelty	Management of existing business operations
Type of Activities	Finding opportunities, risk-taking	Day-to-day operations, resource allocation
Objectives	Growth, disruption, market impact	Stability, sustainability, profitability
Mind-set	Forward-thinking, visionary	Practical, operational, strategic
Approach	Proactive, creative, adaptive	Reactive, systematic, methodical
Risk Tolerance	High risk tolerance	Moderate risk tolerance
Scale	Can range from small to large ventures	Typically focuses on small-scale operations
Time Horizon	Long-term focus on growth and impact	Short to medium-term focus on stability
Innovation	Central to the entrepreneurial process	This may involve incremental improvements
Flexibility	Embraces change and uncertainty	Seeks stability and consistency
Leadership Style	Often requires visionary leadership	May involve more hands-on or managerial style

2.6 Essential Business Skills for Small Business Owners:

Entrepreneurs are expected to possess more abilities than just business acumen. There are a ton of additional topics that an entrepreneur needs whole know about. For instance, the capacity to keep customers or staff from quitting or perhaps the capacity to work hard for the upcoming investment round. An entrepreneur cannot thrive without these abilities. Now let's examine nine essential business skills for entrepreneurs. Certain business skills are essential for any entrepreneur to possess. Some of the key skills are listed below:

a) **Communication skills:** One of the most important fundamental talents for an entrepreneur should possess is the ability to communicate well. This implies that they must be able to communicate effectively and provide clear explanations in a variety of settings, such as putting out office fires, settling disputes with investors, and serving as the de facto point of contact for the majority of significant projects. To put it briefly, founders must be able to communicate with their staff, clients, and investors in a way that fosters understanding and trust. Their company can fail and their ideas might not be comprehended if they are unable to communicate effectively. becoming able to persuade others is a critical component of becoming a successful entrepreneur, and technology cannot replace this ability.

b) **Networking:** Getting to know people who can support an entrepreneur in their business is known as networking. These people might be mentors, advisers, investors, or fellow business owners. Is networking really that crucial? Indeed. Developing relationships is crucial as it can have a knock-on effect on the company's success. An entrepreneur can still establish valuable relationships even if they did not attend a prestigious university. In the end, asking questions about the experiences of others and truly interested in their stories are key components of a successful networking strategy. You may, for instance:

   ✓ Inquire about their travels.
   ✓ Discover their achievements and shortcomings.
   ✓ Discover what motivated them to take the current course of action

- ✓ Get insightful counsel on how they overcame obstacles, built products, recruited investors, dealt with laws and regulations, and other issues.

Which are the best methods to begin networking?

a) Participating in start-up gatherings

b) Organizing events for fellow business owners

c) Giving other founders the time and encouragement they need to expand their businesses.

c) **Capabilities for Leading:** Rank three on our list of entrepreneurship business competencies: Being a leader is a crucial ability for business owners. Managing a business may be challenging, with numerous challenges to face. Nonetheless, a capable team leader can empower their group to meet these obstacles head-on and with purpose. Even large, prosperous businesses have had difficulties, but they are led by capable individuals. The success of an entrepreneur's business depends on their ability to lead. An entrepreneur can look to be a competent leader even though there isn't a clear manual on how to become one. A competent leader, for instance, has a clear vision and self- and team-belief. They have faith in their concept and its potential to help their clients.

d) **Sales:** Being a successful salesperson should be one of an entrepreneur's fundamental talents. Why? Salespeople converse with consumers frequently, so they are familiar with their thoughts and desires. Being in close proximity to the customers allows them to identify issues with the way a business is being conducted. Thus, developing sales skills is crucial to starting a profitable company. A decent product won't sell by itself because there are so many other options available. Even in difficult times, entrepreneurs that work hard and learn how to market will be able to keep their firm relevant. Additionally, selling can assist business owners in dispelling preconceived notions about the market. It aids in their comprehension of what functions well in the actual world and how to advance their company. They will gain knowledge that they might not have otherwise acquired.

e) **Capacity to Accept Criticism:** Has the adage "Doing the same thing over and over again and expecting different results is lunacy" ever occurred to you? Yes, that is accurate! Because of this, business owners must develop their ability to accept criticism from peers, investors, clients, and staff.

You could, after all, be mistaken in a multitude of ways, and occasionally you won't know what to do next. There are numerous approaches to efficiently collect input. For instance, you can solicit input from colleagues, investors, and seasoned business owners, or you can utilize online feedback tools like Survey Sparrow to administer online questionnaires to clients or staff. It's not required that you follow every suggestion. Nonetheless, gathering input will at the very least help you understand what pertinent stakeholders believe about one's company and leadership.

f) **Handling Money:** A fundamental skill for entrepreneurs is having an adequate supply of capital to sustain their business. A company might not succeed if one don't handle their finances well. It might be difficult to launch a business without sufficient cash, even if you have a fantastic idea. The aftermath of COVID-19 remains a major concern, and with concerns of a recession, investment has dried up. Because of this, it is even more crucial for firms to manage their finances carefully. How should I start? Find strategies to reduce spending by first keeping track of where (and how much) money is coming in and going out. One can make wise decisions and prevent financial waste if they have a solid grasp of their finances. Additionally, it's critical to understand how to read financial accounts such as cash flow, balance, and income statements. You can identify areas for savings and areas where you're overspending with the aid of these documents. Possessing the requisite financial knowledge will prevent one from overspending and ensure that their money is spent only where it is required.

g) **Maintaining Focus:** As the business head of their start-up, entrepreneurs have a plethora of tasks to attend to. Hiring an accountant is just as vital to them as seeking financing. They cannot neglect one area of their work because they believe it to be more vital than the other. Because of this, prosperous entrepreneurs are never unclear about their ultimate objectives. They employ a variety of strategies to stay out of the distraction trap, such as filtering off alerts or focus periods. There will occasionally be problems that arise. There are a few things you won't fully understand when you're starting from scratch. Managing many business facets might present challenges for individuals. This is when one organization benefits from maintaining focus on their primary objective. They have to maintain their composure, self-assurance, and goal-focused.

h) **People Management:** What makes this one of the business competencies in entrepreneurship? Working with a diverse group of people with varying backgrounds and skill sets is essential to running a business. Selecting the correct staff is crucial because they have a big influence on a company's performance. Moreover, one has to assign jobs to others because they will not able to complete everything by themselves. Furthermore, employees will feel undervalued and unlikely to want to stay with the company if one micromanages them. Therefore, have faith in the staff members' capacity to do the task at hand. Give the staff the tools and encouragement they require to perform well, and be explicit in communicating one's expectations. Indeed, one can automate this procedure with the use of online survey forms. To illustrate with a few examples:
   - ✓ **Survey on employee empowerment:** Do the staff members have the freedom to choose for themselves at work? These questionnaires will assist you in learning more.
   - ✓ **Form for the training checklist:** Do they have all the tools and procedures needed for your program? Use this template for a training checklist to find out.
   - ✓ **Employee Productivity Questionnaire:** Is there a productive work environment at your place of employment? One can find the answers for this on the employee productivity form.
   - ✓ **Employee professional development survey:** Use this customisable chat poll to create a training program based on the employees' choices.

i) **Having a Growing Mentality:** A growth mind-set is one of the many instances of business talents that we have discussed here, and it will aid entrepreneurs in maintaining focus. Those who have a growth mentality view challenges as chances to improve. They are able to maintain focus and move closer to their objectives as a result. An entrepreneur with a growth mentality is able to view every setback as a learning opportunity. An individual possessing such a mind-set can effectively evaluate and refine ideas during the entrepreneurial journey. Throughout the trip, you'll take use of the possibilities presented to you and look for additional ways to get better. Since beginning a business might be unpredictable, it's critical to have a positive outlook and concentrate on expansion. Entrepreneurs can overcome any obstacles in their path if they have a growth attitude.

2.7 Entrepreneurship Abilities for Companies

Entrepreneurs do more than just start a company and earn profits for themselves. Additionally, they have a big impact on the economy and society by generating jobs and goods and services that raise people's standard of living. However, not everyone has the courage to take on the risk involved in their business or the weight of that obligation. In order to grow a company, meet obstacles head-on, and achieve success, let's examine the top 10 entrepreneurship skills in this post and learn how to develop them. Entrepreneurs that possess these abilities will be better able to spot opportunities, make wise choices, bring their ideas to life, overcome obstacles, and allocate resources wisely in order to prosper.

- ✓ Promoting social change and enhancing lives is the first reason why entrepreneurship skills are important.
- ✓ Creating job chances for other people.
- ✓ Promoting economic expansion and expanding into new markets.
- ✓ Developing innovative concepts and creating useful goods or services to enhance people's quality of life.
- ✓ Providing financial benefits along with chances for professional and personal development.
- ✓ Improving one's ability to operate both independently and cooperatively.
- ✓ Achieving outstanding outcomes and reaching the targeted aims.

2.8 Chapter Summary:

Managing a small business requires you to multitask and maintain concentration on several duties. You may continue on the path to success and maintain focus on the most crucial elements of a business by using these helpful hints and techniques. Managing a small business can be quite challenging. It's simple to forget about key responsibilities during the rush and anxiety of launching an own business. It's the realization of a long-held ambition, but there are certain difficulties that you wouldn't encounter in a regular 9–5 office job. Managing a small business is all about making one's daily responsibilities more efficient so that one can devote more time and effort to the things that are most important to become an entrepreneur.

2.9 *Multiple Choice Questions*

1. Entrepreneurship in companies can lead to:
   a) Innovation and competitiveness
   b) Avoiding growth opportunities
   c) Stagnation in business practices
   d) Resistance to customer needs
   Answer: a) Innovation and competitiveness
2. Entrepreneurship contributes to economic growth by:
   a) Increasing government dependency
   b) Creating new jobs and businesses
   c) Discouraging competition
   d) Avoiding innovation
   Answer: b) Creating new jobs and businesses
3. Which of the following is a key characteristic of small businesses?
   a) Unlimited resources
   b) High employee turnover
   c) Personalized customer service
   d) Global market dominance
   Answer: c) Personalized customer service

2.10 *Short Type Questions*

1. What is the significance of risk-taking in entrepreneurship?
2. How is small business management different from general management?
3. How does entrepreneurship contribute to job creation?

2.11 *Essay Type Questions*

1. Evaluate the relationship between entrepreneurial mind-set and small business success.

2. Analyse how the goals of an entrepreneur differ from those of a small business manager. Provide examples to support your argument.
3. Compare and contrast the management approaches of small businesses versus large corporations.

2.13 Mini- Case Study

A local bakery with limited space and staff struggles to balance daily operations while expanding its product line. The study will cover fundamental management areas like inventory control, staffing, workflow optimization, and customer service management.

Question:

- What are the key operational management challenges that the bakery faces?
- How can the bakery improve its inventory and staff management to increase efficiency?
- How does customer service impact the success of the bakery, and what measures can be taken to enhance it?

2.14 References

1. Halvorson, M. (2021). *The small business start-up guide* (4th ed.). Sourcebooks.
2. Hatten, T. S. (2020). *Small business management: Entrepreneurship and beyond* (7th ed.). Cengage Learning.
3. Burns, P. (2016). *Entrepreneurship and small business* (4th ed.). Palgrave Macmillan.

Chapter -3: Starting Procedure of a Small Business

3.1 Introduction:

There are several processes involved in starting a business in the United States, including market research, legal concerns, writing a business plan, obtaining capital, and designing a marketing strategy. It also necessitates choosing a company's name, structure, location, taxation, and registration. These are the essential steps in launching a business, along with crucial elements that business owners should think about. India is a land of opportunity, and the nation has well-planned tactics and appropriate ways to help you realize the ambition of starting and running a successful business. Even though launching a firm can be difficult, things have gotten easier recently because of efficient operations and work processes. As a result, choosing to launch a business in India will pay you more than you could have imagined.

3.2 Overview of Businesses in India:

Over time, the business landscape in India underwent a paradigm shift that opened up a plethora of opportunities for the country's emerging and expanding economic sectors. Without a question, the Indian government was instrumental in reforming Indian enterprises by providing opportunities and motivating them to seize them. With the implementation of macroeconomic, financial, tax, and market easing measures, India completely redesigned the country's business environment. Consequently, the potential for conducting business in India has increased significantly. With the support of the Made in India initiative, an increasing number of businesses are joining the market with the goal of becoming more operationally and commercially successful as well as building their own brands. Doing business in India is no longer a laborious process. Rather, the firm expands globally and the schemes and efforts make it easier for everyone to access sources. Given these details, it is obvious that Indian companies still have a long way to go before they can fully utilize their advantage.

3.3 Types of Businesses to Start in India

India is open to receiving new business ventures of any form. There is no limit to the industries you can choose from and launch a business in: automotive, finance, cement, jewelry, gemstones, healthcare, IT, banking, insurance, media, oil and gas, real estate, textiles, tourism, hospitality, agriculture, pharmaceuticals, food, and so on. Thus, depending on the industry, as a firm, you can either offer a product or a service. On the other hand, you can launch the following platforms and enterprises in India:

a) **Sole Proprietary Company:** A solitary proprietorship is run and owned by just one individual. This group includes minor merchants and tradesmen. This type of business recognizes registration through service or GST registration.
b) **Partnership firm:** As specified in the partnership deed, a partnership firm is a type of business in which two or more people decide to collaborate and oversee the day-to-day operations of the company. Forming a partnership is a feasible solution that requires less complexity, particularly for home-based firms.

c) **Limited Liability Partnership:** With regard to the partners' liabilities, a Limited Liability Partnership is not the same as a regular partnership. This protects partners connected to the company from other partners' carelessness, wrongdoing, and incapacity so long as it doesn't destroy the Partnership.

d) **One Person Company (OPC):** An OPC offers the business owner two advantages. Being a lone proprietor comes first, followed by corporate promotion. With the exception of equity funding and providing employee stock option plans, the individual can benefit from the formation of a company.

e) **Private Limited Company:** In India, companies are the most often used type of business structure. You can benefit from capital, limited liability, and drawing in the right purchases by establishing a company. The Ministry of Corporate Affairs, responsible for government oversight, requires firms to conduct meetings and submit annual reports.

f) **Public Limited Company:** Compared to a Private Limited Company, a Public Limited Company undoubtedly offers more benefits. These businesses are free to draw in investors, go public via initial public offerings, and have freedom.

These businesses are ideal for corporations with a distinct viewpoint and more room for expansion. SAIL, GAIL, BHEL, IOCL, and a few others are a few examples. These thus are the six categories of enterprises that can be founded in India. It is advised that you carefully consider all of the characteristics, benefits, and drawbacks of each business form before choosing one and moving on with the formation process.

3.4 Why Is It a Good Idea to Set Up Business in India?

India is currently in a highly advanced phase. As a result, it is becoming increasingly feasible to establish a presence in global marketplaces. The Indian government creates an atmosphere that is conducive to business so that all organizations can flourish and realize their goals. Because of this, it is now more practical for companies to establish themselves in India in order to preserve their stability and market expansion. Furthermore, organizations can have the chance to work and develop in the global market. Let's examine the top five factors that demonstrate the benefits of establishing a company in India:

a) **Ease of Doing Business:** As previously said, the market and governmental regulations have simplified the process of launching a business. The government is doing much to assist those who are beginning businesses by easing the process through the passage of business-friendly regulations, market liberalization, and streamlined registration procedures.
b) **Rise in Market Demand:** The Indian market has continuously seen strong demand. Everyone in India needs a variety of stuff, from luxury goods to necessities. Given the rate of population growth, there is a growing need for the products, which has encouraged firms to seize the opportunity to expand into related industries and meet market demands.
c) **Cost-Effectiveness**: Compared to other nations, starting a business in India is far less expensive. The advantages of having access to land, labour, electricity, and infrastructure can help you increase production levels. By now, you should be able to realize economies of scale, which will lower the production costs overall.
d) **Offer a Sustainable Business Environment**: India is a developing country with a plethora of business opportunities. As such, the Indian market offers a sustainable environment that allows any kind of business to grow and thrive on a large scale. India has flipped the tables, making it more business-friendly by providing for the future.
e) **Employment scope:** This rationale stems from the preceding one. By creating a sustainable business environment, the companies raise the standard of living and give job possibilities to those in the industry.

3.5 Starting a Business – What are all should be considered?

Beginning a business presents a number of common issues for business firms. Making decisions about the business is necessary when it is just starting out. Here are a few fundamental things to think about while launching a business:

a) **Choosing a Business Line:** Any entrepreneur starting a new firm must first determine the kind of business to be operated. It is best to enter a growing business where there is a greater chance of making money. In this context, the entrepreneur's technical expertise and enthusiasm for creating a certain product are equally crucial.

b) **Firm Size:** The firm's size describes the scope of its activities. If an entrepreneur has the required skills and cash and is convinced that there will be a high demand for the proposed product over time, then a large-scale firm can be established. If there are significant dangers and unstable market conditions, a business should be launched on a small or medium-sized scale.

c) **Type of Ownership:** A business organization might be a single proprietorship, partnership, or joint stock company, among other types of ownership. The selection of an appropriate ownership structure is contingent upon various elements, including but not limited to capital requirements, owner liability, profit distribution, and transferability of interests.

d) **Business Enterprise Location:** When starting a business, the location of the plant is a crucial consideration. While choosing a location, it's crucial to consider the availability of labor and raw materials as well as power supplies and services like banking, warehousing, transportation, and communication.

e) **Financing Decisions:** Financing deals with supplying the funds required to launch and maintain the proposed firm. Investments in current and fixed assets both require capital. A thorough financial planning process is necessary to ascertain the amount, source, and distribution of funds.

f) **Physical Facilities:** One of the most crucial things to take into account at the beginning of the firm is the availability of physical facilities, such as buildings, machinery, and support services. The choice about this component will be based on the type and scale of the company, the funding source, and the manufacturing method.

g) **Plant Layout:** A plant layout is a blueprint that illustrates how physical facilities, including machinery and industrial equipment, are arranged. The entrepreneur should draw it after determining the scope of the business and the actual spaces that need to be purchased.

h) **Competent and Devoted Workers:** Nowadays, a company's most important asset is its people capital. Every company relies on the skill and dedication of its employees to carry out a variety of tasks in order to efficiently and effectively transform material and monetary resources into the intended results.

i) **Tax Planning:** All businesses are required to pay specific taxes that are imposed by the government. Both morally and legally, tax planning and management aimed at minimizing tax liabilities are permissible. The tax liabilities under different tax laws and how it affects business decisions must be taken into account beforehand by the entrepreneur.

j) **Enterprise Launching:** Following the decisions made regarding the aforementioned factors, the entrepreneur can proceed with the actual enterprise launch. This entails assembling a variety of resources, completing the required legal formalities, kicking off the production process, and launching the sales promotion campaign.

3.6 Steps in Starting and Planning the Business:

You must thoroughly research the background before launching the company. By background, we mean having the will to launch a business and see it through to the end, regardless of the challenges. The 12-step start-up approach that will assist you in transforming the business concept into a successful execution is provided below:

1. Consider and select a business concept: It's important to consider all the options and make a decision before taking control of the firm. Since there are a lot of profitable company ideas out there, break them down, make guidelines, get advice, look into concepts, and weigh all the options before launching the venture.

2. Perform Market Research: The next stage after receiving a company concept is to conduct market research to see whether your goals are appropriate. To gain a deep understanding of the specific industry, one might begin by looking at their possible partners and competitors. Prioritizing market research is essential and should be done first.

3. Acquire abilities and Training: Following the first two phases, the third crucial step is to get the expertise, training, and applicable abilities that can make your company a billionaire. It is essential to take specialist training classes or gain the necessary experience working for various clients and companies before launching a firm. No one knows your business better than you, thus your prior knowledge and experience in the particular market can help you develop new perspectives for it.

4. Document the Business Plan: Because there is so much to learn at each step, it is crucial to record the ways in which your business plan is changing, including feasibility studies, end-to-end project reports, and other specifics. You can display it more effectively and add a polished touch to your ideas and thoughts by creating a comprehensive document plan. This will also increase the number of potential customers who are curious about your strategy and ready you for future behavior.

5. Funding the company: Money is the company's lifeline. The sources of the start-up capital must be decided upon by the firms. This process entails gathering estimates, doing financial calculations, and determining dependable business funding options. Banks, financial institutions, cooperatives, crowdfunding, angel investors, venture capitalists, and self-funding are a few of the main sources.

6. Begin with the Development of Your Product or Service: Now that the five important phases have been discussed, it is time to build the product and service and establish the goal of a company. Making a checklist of the things you need to do to identify a manufacturer, decide on pricing, design the product, and create a trial run for the service or product is crucial when you're producing it.

7. Assemble your team: When your company is first starting out, you will be the only employee. Eventually, you'll need a group of teams to assist you in growing your company. The members of the team are the freelancer, employee, or partner who best suits your requirements.

8. Choose your place: Choosing a location is one of the most important things you can do when launching a business. The target market that best fits your business operations and your skills are among the area's factors. It can be a tiny store, a concession stand, or a functioning office. Given how important the location is to your firm, there should be no compromising.

9. Register yourself as a business: At this point, you should establish your brand and identify yourself in the market after deciding on the product, location, and financial details. The first step towards launching your business is completing the registration process, which entails all the formalities of founding a firm.

10. Establish and manage a website: The global epidemic has already ushered in an online era. You can keep your brand visible online and facilitate direct product and service ordering and payment processes with a website. Additionally, it will strengthen consumer trust and help you establish a brand in the industry.

11. Begin with making sales: The future of your company lies in this phase. Even once you've gotten started, it's critical to make money by using various approaches and tactics to attract customers. Your firm can survive by identifying its target market, expanding its clientele, running advertisements, building sales funnels, sampling, sales promotion, and any other tactics that turn leads into purchases.

12. Develop and expand your company: No company can last for very long without a growth plan. Consequently, the company must explore new avenues for growth and expansion in order to ensure a more prosperous and sustainable future. Levelling up allows the company to launch a new product, extend its offers, buy other companies, establish new target markets, develop marketing strategies, and cultivate positive client connections. In-depth research, recruiting qualified candidates, producing top-notch goods, and going above and beyond are just a few other tactics that can help you create the empire of your dreams.

3.7 Process of Registering a Business in India:

In order to stay out of trouble with the law, businesses in India must go through a registration process that comprises several regulations. The first step in starting a business and developing your plan of action is registering your company. The essential actions that must be taken when registering a business in India are as follows:

a) **Choose a name that is appropriate for the company:** Choosing and selecting a name for your firm is the first step. Since the name of your company represents who you are, choosing a name for it is essential. A name that is memorable, powerful, and in line with your goals should be chosen. You must make sure that your name doesn't already belong to another brand or business when you register your company name. Once the inspection is complete, you can register your company name with the Registrar.

b) **Application for the Director Identification Number (DIN) and Digital Signature Certificate (DSC):** In accordance with the Information Technology Act of 2000, the company is required to utilize digital signatures on any electronic documents that are presented. In order to prove that the documents are legitimate, the company must apply for the Digital Signature Certificate. This will support the process of guaranteeing the security and legitimacy of the papers that the individual files online. In a similar vein, the person designated as a director of the company is given a Director Identification Number. To register, the individual must apply using the DR-3 form and acquire the registration number.

c) **Document preparation:** Depending on the kind of business you intend to pursue, there are several paperwork that must be ready when registering a firm. Depending on whether you want to incorporate as a partnership firm, private limited company, OPC, or another type of organization, there are several sets of paperwork and procedures. It is advised to make a list of the necessary documents that must be attached during the registration procedure in advance.

d) **Sign in to the website and complete the form:** You can register your company or the business after you've finished the preliminary procedures and prepared the necessary paperwork. As the procedure is now conducted online, you must complete the registration application.

e) **Submit the documents:** The last and final step in the registration process is to submit the documents in PDF format after completing the application form. You must pay the registration fees at this stage. Upon payment completion, you will receive a registration number that you may use to monitor the status of your registration. Following a comprehensive review and cross-examination of the documents, your business will be successfully registered in the business books.

3.8 Prerequisite Documents for Registration:

Understanding the paperwork needed for registration is crucial before launching a firm. Each document serves as official documentation to launch your business and fulfill all legal criteria in India. Businesses have varied documentation requirements, as stated in the registration process. You must maintain an eye on documents that are appropriately created. The following is a list of common documents needed for registration:

- ✓ **Founder's Agreement:** A formal contract signed by the company's founder is known as the "founder's agreement." Both co-founders are necessary if there are any. Photographs, Pan cards, and ID proof details of the company's directors, partners, or proprietor are also included.
- ✓ **Certificate of incorporation:** This legal document establishes the business and renders your business formation legitimate is the Certificate of Incorporation.
- ✓ **Business PAN Card:** In order to register, the business's PAN card is a necessary document.
- ✓ **Tax Identification Number (TIN):** The TIN is an 11-digit number that is exclusive to each firm and is used to identify it.
- ✓ **Digital Signature Certificate (DSC)**: This certificate serves as legal documentation allowing the business to use its signature on official documents.
- ✓ **Goods and Services Taxpayer Identification Number (GSTIN):** Businesses are required to have a GSTIN, which is a 15-digit number based on a taxpayer's PAN.
- ✓ **Address Proof:** Utility bills, bank statements, or any oth er document that can serve as verification of the registere d office's legal address.
- ✓ **Additional pertinent documents:** You'll need to set up the other related documents based on the business organization you choose.

3.9 Benefits of Registering a Business in India:

India offers numerous advantages to organizations seeking to benefit from the impacts of registration, thanks to the development of the internet and a seamless registration process. Let's examine a few advantages of completing the registration process:

- ✓ Simplicity of transferability or joint ownership of the company
- ✓ Simplicity of tax registration and bank account setup.
- ✓ Helps the company obtain money

- ✓ A reduction in a number of tax exemptions
- ✓ Makes doing business with firms easier
- ✓ Availability of resources and clients
- ✓ A hassle-free method of operation

3.10 Chapter Summary

Starting a small business demands persistence, hard work, and patience. If you're willing to put in the effort, it can be an excellent way to achieve your goals. Be sure to conduct thorough research, develop a robust business plan, and be prepared to adapt as needed. Remember to maintain organization and focus once your firm is up and running in order to expand it further. Making the brave decision to launch your own small business is only the beginning of your entrepreneurial journey. India's MSME Ministry is in charge of small and start-up companies as well as internet businesses. MSME maintains offices throughout all seven Union Territories and all of India's states. The ministry's licensing, rules, and regulations apply to MSMEs. It creates and puts into action a range of strategies and programs meant to promote entrepreneurship. This ministry frequently releases announcements about programs like offering money to prospective companies on favourable terms.

3.11 Multiple Choice Questions

1. What is the first step in starting a small business?
   a) Hiring employees
   b) Writing a business plan
   c) Registering the business
   d) Marketing the business
   Answer: b) Writing a business plan
2. What percentage of businesses in India are classified as micro, small, and medium enterprises (MSMEs)?
   a) 25%
   b) 50%
   c) 95%
   d) 99%
   Answer: d) 99%
3. Which type of business is most popular among small business entrepreneurs in India?
   a) Sole Proprietorship
   b) Partnership

c) Private Limited Company
d) Public Limited Company
Answer: a) Sole Proprietorship

3.12 Short Type Questions

1. Mention two key industries where small businesses are prominent in India.
2. What factors influence the choice of a business type in India?
3. How does business registration enhance credibility with customers?

3.13 Essay Type Questions

1. Discuss how business registration enables access to formal credit and funding opportunities in India.
2. Compare the registration process for different types of businesses in India
3. Outline the key steps involved in starting a small business and explain their significance.

3.14 Mini- Case Study:

Starting Procedure of a Small Business: An individual decides to start a pet grooming business. The case will explore the necessary steps involved, such as obtaining licenses, registering the business, finding a location, sourcing equipment, and hiring initial staff.

Question:

- What are the essential legal and administrative steps involved in starting the pet grooming business?
- What challenges did the entrepreneur face during the start-up phase, and how were they overcome?
- How did the entrepreneur secure the necessary equipment and hire staff?

3.15 References

1. Sharma, S. (2019). *Start-up India: Policies, opportunities and challenges*. Sage Publications.
2. Gupta, R. (2020). *Guide to company law in India*. Taxmann Publications.
3. Panagariya, A. (2021). *Doing business in India: A guide to success* (2nd ed.). Oxford University Press.

Chapter - 4 : Develop a Feasibility Plan

4.1 Introduction

Even on a bad day, navigating the world of small business can be an exhilarating task. You'll be given a lot of goals, most of which you will disregard, all of which are on various approaches with various boundaries. Financial viability is one of these checkboxes that will appear on your screen of crucial issues that you will overlook. The assessment of a project or business's financial viability involves figuring out whether it can be profitable and produce a high enough return on investment. Although it sounds fancy, consider financial viability as a way to determine if a concept has the potential to be profitable. It's similar to giving a project or company concept in your thoughts a test run to see if it may be profitable. You will examine expenses, prospective revenue, and all other financial aspects to determine whether your idea is a money pit or a gold mine.

4.2 What is meant by a Feasibility Study?

A feasibility study aims to ascertain the practicality, viability, and likelihood of success of a proposed project, business endeavor, or initiative by a thorough and methodical examination and review. The process entails a comprehensive analysis of multiple elements, including those connected to finances, technology, operations, law, the environment, and the market, in order to determine the project's viability and merit. A feasibility study's main objective is to give stakeholders the knowledge and understanding they need to decide whether to move forward with the project, give up on it, or make the required changes to increase its chances of success.

4.3 Distinctions Between a Business Strategy and a Feasibility Study

Feasibility studies and business plans are both crucial for developing and accessing a business or project, but they serve different roles and are created at different stages. The key differences between a business plan and a feasibility study are as follows:

1. **Disparities in Objective**
   - ✓ **Feasibility Study:** During the initial phases of project development or company planning, feasibility studies are carried out. Their main goal is to decide if a project or company idea is feasible and ought to be developed. The main goal of feasibility studies is to evaluate the project's possible risks, difficulties, and opportunities.
   - ✓ **Business Plan:** Following the completion of the feasibility study and the determination that the project is feasible, business plans are written. A business plan is meant to provide a detailed blueprint for how the company will be set up, run, and expanded. It acts as a guide for the company's future and is frequently utilized to obtain funding.
2. **Disparities in Timing:**
   - ✓ **Feasibility Study:** To determine a project's or company idea's potential viability, feasibility studies

are carried out early on. They support stakeholders in determining whether to proceed with the project.

- ✓ **Business Plan:** After a feasibility study concludes that the project is viable and worthwhile, business plans are usually written. They offer a road plan for the company's real operations and expansion.

3. **Variations in the Audience**
   - ✓ **Feasibility Study:** Project stakeholders, financiers, and decision-makers who must decide whether to move forward with the project are the main recipients of a feasibility study.
   - ✓ **Business Plan:** Business plans serve as a means of disseminating the company's goals and tactics to a broader group of people, such as prospective partners, lenders, employees, and investors.

In conclusion, a business plan is a comprehensive document that describes how a business will be operated, whereas a feasibility study is an initial evaluation of a project's potential success. The business plan offers a detailed strategy for the continuous operation and expansion of the company, while the feasibility study assists in determining whether one should be created.

4.4 Feasibility Study vs Pre-Feasibility Study:

Let us now examine the principal distinctions between a feasibility study and a prefeasibility study:

a) **Goal and Range:** Both a feasibility study and a prefeasibility study are essential for project appraisal, although they have different functions. The prefeasibility study is usually the first step in the evaluation procedure. Its main objective is to offer an early assessment of a project's likelihood of success. It assists interested parties in determining if devoting more funds to a thorough feasibility study is worthwhile. A feasibility study, on the other hand, examines the project's viability from the technical, financial, operational, and market aspects in far more detail. It seeks to offer a thorough comprehension of whether the project is viable and worthwhile.

b) **Detail Level:** The degree of detail covered by the two studies is one of their main differences. A prefeasibility analysis provides a high-level overview of the project by analysing variables such as market demand, technical specifications, and approximate cost estimates. It gives you enough details to decide whether to proceed or not at first. A feasibility study, on the other hand, goes into further detail and offers exact financial estimates, risk assessments, engineering specifications, and a thorough business strategy. It aims to evaluate the project's viability from every angle possible.

c) **Implications for Cost and Resources:** Compared to a full feasibility study, a prefeasibility study often requires fewer resources and is less expensive to undertake. It serves as an economical filter to weed out initiatives that won't work out early on in the assessment process. A feasibility study necessitates a greater investment of time, money, and resources because it is a more thorough process than the prefeasibility stage of a project. A feasibility study is a more involved procedure appropriate for projects that have shown a higher possibility of success during the prefeasibility assessment, whereas a prefeasibility study aids in the efficient allocation of resources by concentrating solely on the most promising initiatives.

4.5 Advantages of Conducting a Feasibility Study:

There are many advantages to doing a feasibility study, which is why it is a crucial stage in the decision-making process for any project, commercial endeavour, or initiative. The following are the main benefits of carrying out a feasibility study:

a) **Risk Assessment:** A project's possible hazards and difficulties might be found with the aid of feasibility studies. Through a comprehensive analysis of technical, financial, operational, and market-related factors, interested parties can identify risk hotspots and devise effective mitigation or management plans.

b) **Making Decisions:** By giving decision-makers vital information, feasibility studies enable them to decide whether to move forward with a project or not. These investigations provide a foundation for decisions about what is viable and what is not, saving money on projects that are not worthwhile.

c) **Resource Allocation:** Stakeholders can more effectively allocate resources by evaluating a project's viability. By allocating resources to projects with a higher chance of success, they can avoid overinvesting in ones with little potential.

d) **Financial Planning:** Detailed cost and financial estimations are included in feasibility studies. Having this financial data is crucial if you want to get loans, investors, or other funding sources. It aids in the development of a strong business case.

e) **Market Insight:** Research on market viability sheds light on consumer demand, industry trends, and rivalry. This data is essential for creating goods and services that satisfy consumer demands and for creating winning marketing plans.

f) **Optimised Design:** Technical feasibility studies guarantee the viability of a project's design and technical specifications. They ensure that the project can be carried out according to schedule and assist in avoiding expensive design errors.

g) **Legal and Regulatory Compliance:** Legal and regulatory issues may be found through feasibility studies. This lowers the possibility of future legal issues by enabling the development of strategies to navigate and abide by pertinent rules and regulations.

h) **Increased Project Viability**: Project plans may be improved and adjusted as a result of feasibility studies, increasing their likelihood of success. Potential problems are ensured to be addressed proactively through this iterative procedure.

i) **Confidence among Investors and Stakeholders:** Prospective investors and stakeholders are more likely to have faith in the project when they perceive that an extensive feasibility study has been carried out. Obtaining money and help may become simpler as a result.

j) **Long-Term Planning:** In addition to determining a project's short-term viability, feasibility studies also support long-term planning. They offer perceptions into a company's or initiative's prospects for expansion and sustainability.

In conclusion, carrying out a feasibility study is an important stage in the creation of a project. It offers a methodical way to evaluate a project's viability, control risks, come to wise judgments, find funding, and create the conditions for a profitable endeavour. Beyond helping with early decision-making, a feasibility study is beneficial for a project or business's overall performance and long-term viability.

4.6 Elements of a Feasibility Investigation

Usually comprising multiple essential elements, a feasibility study offers a thorough assessment of a project, business endeavor, or initiative. These elements support interested parties in making defensible choices regarding the viability and feasibility of the project. The following are the major elements of a feasibility study:

- ✓ **Executive Summary:** This section offers a succinct synopsis of the whole feasibility study. It contains a succinct overview of the project's goals, major conclusions, and suggestions. Making decisions is facilitated by its fast reference nature.
- ✓ **Project Description:** The aims, objectives, and scope of the project are described in this section. It identifies the opportunity or problem that the initiative is trying to tackle. It also lists the stakeholders and the location of the project.
- ✓ **Market Analysis:** This method evaluates the target market's willingness to pay for the good or service. Target consumer information, market size, growth potential, rivalry, and market trends are all included. This element aids in determining whether the project has a feasible market.
- ✓ **Technological Feasibility:** This stage looks at the project's technological specifications. It evaluates if the required tools, resources, and technology are already in place or can be created. It also points out any technological issues that could require attention.
- ✓ **Operational Feasibility:** This section assesses the project's ability to be carried out and run. It contains information about the schedules for projects, workflow, manpower needs, and operational procedures. This part

aids in comprehending the day-to-day operations of the project.

- ✓ **Financial Feasibility:** Detailed financial estimates and analysis are part of the crucial financial feasibility component. It addresses topics like cash flow analysis, revenue forecasts, cost estimations, startup expenses, and return on investment computations. It evaluates the project's prospective profitability and financial viability.
- ✓ **Legal and Regulatory Analysis:** In this phase, the requirements pertaining to law and regulation that could affect the project are examined. It indicates licenses, permits, or compliance problems that require attention. It is imperative to comprehend and tackle legal and regulatory concerns in order to prevent any potential roadblocks.
- ✓ **Risk Assessment:** This section of the project's evaluation identifies possible dangers and difficulties. It assesses these risks' likelihood and consequences and makes recommendations for risk-reduction tactics. Risks can be associated with the market, finances, technology, operations, or external variables.
- ✓ **Recommendations and Conclusion:** The feasibility study provides a concise summary of the results in this part, along with specific recommendations derived from the evaluation. It frequently concludes with a statement on the project's viability and worth, as well as recommendations for revision or abandonment.
- ✓ **Appendices**: Additional supporting paperwork and data, including technical specifications, market research studies, detailed financial spreadsheets, and any other pertinent information, are included in the appendices. These give stakeholders a more comprehensive reference.

When taken as a whole, the primary elements of a feasibility study offer an extensive evaluation of a project's viability from several perspectives, guaranteeing that decision-makers have a complete grasp of the project's potential, risks, and advantages.

4.7 Feasibility Study Examples

Now let's examine some instances of feasibility studies for various enterprises and endeavours:

- ✓ **Real Estate Development:** In a developing urban region, a real estate developer is thinking about building a residential apartment complex. Market demand, location, zoning laws, building costs, prospective rental income, and the project's financial sustainability would all be evaluated in a feasibility study.
- ✓ **Manufacturing Plant Expansion:** Constructing a new production facility is one way that a manufacturing company plans to grow. A variety of criteria, including labor, infrastructure, equipment needs, site availability, environmental impact, and the expansion's financial viability, would be assessed as part of the feasibility study.
- ✓ **Small Business Start-up:** An entrepreneur is determining whether opening a tiny restaurant in a particular area is feasible. The local market, rivals, target consumer demographics, start-up costs, legal requirements, and financial estimates for the first few years of business would all be examined in the feasibility study.
- ✓ **Renewable Energy Project:** Building a solar power plant is something that a renewable energy company is thinking about doing. The site's solar exposure, the viability of connecting to the grid, the cost of the equipment, the revenue from energy sales, the influence on the environment, and the project's overall return on investment would all be evaluated in the feasibility study.
- ✓ **Healthcare Facility Expansion:** In order to accommodate the increasing needs of its patients, a hospital is considering expanding. The necessary medical equipment, staffing requirements, regulatory compliance, funding sources, and the expected patient load would all be evaluated as part of the feasibility study.
- ✓ **Tourism Development:** Building a new hotel and recreational amenities is something that a tourist destination is thinking of doing. The area's attraction to

tourists, rivalry with already-established enterprises, building expenses, anticipated occupancy rates, and potential tourism earnings would all be assessed in the feasibility study.

- ✓ **Non-profit Program Expansion:** A non-profit wants to increase the scope of its community service initiatives. The demand for the programs, financing sources, volunteer availability, operational costs, and the effect of the expansion on the organization's mission and objectives would all be evaluated as part of the feasibility study.
- ✓ **E-commerce Start-up:** A business owner intends to start an online store. The feasibility study will look at predicted sales income and profitability, marketing strategy, competitive analysis, website development expenses, and market demand.

These examples show how feasibility studies are carried out across a variety of disciplines and sectors to assess the viability and potential success of several projects and initiatives. A feasibility study's particular elements and areas of concentration will change based on the project's objectives and nature.

4.8 Steps in Conducting a Feasibility Study:

Let us now imagine that we are going to compose a feasibility study. Let's see what needs to be done to prepare the final report.

- ✓ **Perform an Initial Analysis:** Start by performing a preliminary assessment of the goals and extent of the project. This step entails outlining the opportunity or problem that the initiative seeks to address. Make sure the project's objectives are precise and well-defined.
- ✓ **Examine the Technical Details:** Analyse the project's technical components in great depth. Analyse the resources, equipment, and technology that are needed. Check if the technical needs of the project can be met in an efficient manner.
- ✓ **Conduct a Commercial Analysis:** Examine the project's commercial features in-depth. In this step, the demand for the product or service is evaluated, and the market's size, competitors, consumer wants, and trends are examined. Conduct a viability study of the project.

- ✓ **Create a Projected Income Statement:** For the project, prepare a thorough projected income statement. This covers cash flow analysis, revenue forecasting, spending predictions, and start-up cost estimation. Determine the project's financial viability by calculating the return on investment (ROI), the investment's internal rate of return (IRR), and the future cash flows' net present value (NPV).
- ✓ **Create a Day-Zero Balance Sheet:** Create a balance sheet that shows the financial status of the project from the beginning (day zero). Before the project starts, a clear picture of its financial status should be provided by accounting for all assets, liabilities, and equity.
- ✓ **Examine Various Alternatives for Feasibility:** Investigate a range of options and situations to see whether the project is feasible. Examine various strategies, tools, or business models to determine which is the most practical. Think about how these options might affect the project's outcome. Be mindful of possible hazards.
- ✓ **Decide whether to proceed or not:** Make an informed choice on whether to move forward with the project (a "Go" decision) or abandon it (a "No-Go" decision) based on the analysis and data gathered throughout the feasibility study. Make sure the choice is in line with the objectives of the project and the data that was gathered for the analysis.

By following these steps, you can perform a feasibility study in an organized manner and make sure that all pertinent project components are carefully evaluated and taken into account before determining whether the project is feasible.

4.9 Chapter Summary

To sum up, a feasibility study is a crucial component of any project, enterprise, or business endeavour. It acts as the vital link between an idea and a well-reasoned choice. Stakeholders can obtain a thorough grasp of a project's feasibility by adhering to a methodical procedure that involves a preliminary analysis, technical assessment, commercial evaluation, financial predictions, and a careful consideration of alternatives. By using a feasibility study, business owners can make informed-decisions that helps them to evaluate the market demand, technological feasibility, operational requirements, financial viability, and potential dangers. For any type of project—real estate development, new product introduction, manufacturing expansion, IT system upgrade, or otherwise—a feasibility study aids in risk assessment, effective resource allocation, and, eventually, the accomplishment of the project's objectives. It's crucial to keep in mind that a well-executed feasibility study not only helps a project get approved but also lays the groundwork for its long-term success. It provides stakeholders with the assurance that the project is founded on solid planning and analysis. For individuals who aim to transform creative concepts into tangible projects, the feasibility study serves as a crucial guide amidst intricate obstacles and prospects.

4.10 Multiple Choice Questions

1. Feasibility studies help entrepreneurs by:
   A. Ensuring immediate profits
   B. Attracting skilled employees
   C. Providing data for informed decision-making
   D. Eliminating competitors
   Answer: C. Providing data for informed decision-making
2. Which of the following is NOT a key element of a feasibility study?
   A. Technical feasibility
   B. Financial feasibility
   C. Market feasibility
   D. Employee satisfaction
   Answer: D. Employee satisfaction
3. Which of the following is part of the feasibility study process?
   A. Conducting market research
   B. Launching a pilot project
   C. Negotiating contracts with clients
   D. Designing product packaging
   Answer: A. Conducting market research

4.11 Short Type Questions

1. Define a feasibility study in the context of business planning.
2. What are the key elements of a feasibility study?
3. Why is data collection and analysis important in a feasibility study?

4.12 Essay Type Questions

1. Outline the key steps involved in conducting a feasibility study. Explain how each step contributes to evaluating the business idea.
2. Analyse the advantages of conducting a pre-feasibility study before proceeding with a full feasibility study.
3. Discuss the key components of a feasibility study and how each contributes to determining a business's potential for success.

4.13 Mini- Case Study: Develop a Feasibility Plan

A person interested in starting a yoga studio conducts a feasibility study. The study includes analysing the target market, evaluating competition, assessing financial needs, and determining if the business can be successful in the proposed location.

Question:

- How did the entrepreneur assess the market demand for the yoga studio?
- What factors contributed to the success or failure of the feasibility study?
- What data would be most critical to collect when evaluating the potential location for the yoga studio?

4.14 References

1. Von Rosing, M., von Scheel, H., & Scheer, A.-W. (2014). *The complete business process handbook*. Morgan Kaufmann.
2. David, F. R., & David, F. R. (2019). *Strategic management: Concepts and cases* (16th ed.). Pearson.
3. Mehta, R. (2020). *Feasibility studies for small enterprises: Guiding entrepreneurs toward sound decisions*. Springer.

Chapter - 5: Preparation of Business Plan for Small Business

5.1 Introduction
5.2 Business Plan – What is it?
5.3 Steps in Business Plan:
5.4 Simple Plan vs Detailed Plan
5.5 How to Choose the Right Business Plan?
5.6 Is Order of the Business Plan Important?
5.7 Traditional Vs Lean Business Plans:
5.8 How to write a Business Plan Step-by-Step?
5.9 How to Prepare a Business Plan:
5.10 Preparing a Business Plan for a Lean Startup
5.11 Writing a Business Plan for Loan:
5.12 Key Points in Composing a Business Plan:
5.13 Sources for Business Plan Writing
5.14 Chapter Summary
5.15 Multiple choice questions
5.16 Short type questions
5.17 Essay type questions
5.18 Mini- Case Study
5.19 References

5.1 Introduction

A business plan is a written document that outlines an organization's goals and the strategies to achieve them. It is valuable for both start-ups and established businesses. A well-crafted business plan is crucial for attracting potential lenders and investors. Writing and following a thoughtfully developed business plan offers numerous benefits. Business plans help established companies stay on course and in line with their expansion goals. The main elements of a successful business plan will be discussed in this article, along with writing tips. Any new business should have a business plan in place before beginning operations. Before contemplating granting a loan or contributing funds to start-up companies, banks and venture capital firms frequently request to see a business plan. Having a business plan aids a company in maintaining focus on its objectives, even in cases where it does not require further investment. According to University of Oregon research, companies that have a plan have a much higher chance of obtaining funding than those that don't. Additionally, businesses that have a business strategy expand thirty percent quicker than those that don't. In an ideal world, a business plan would be evaluated and revised on a regular basis to account for goals accomplished or changes in course. An established company using a different approach can even come up with a whole new plan. Creating and following a well-thought-out business strategy offers numerous benefits. It provides a mechanism for obtaining unbiased feedback from reliable outsiders, identifies possible roadblocks to achievement, and permits thorough evaluation of ideas prior to major investment. The executive team of a company may also benefit from having a business plan to keep them in sync with regard to strategic priorities and action items.

5.2 Business Plan – What is it?

A business plan is a written statement of an organization's objectives that includes the budget, schedule, and strategies required to reach those objectives. A mission statement and information about the particular goods or services provided might also be included. A business plan may highlight several time periods based on the objectives and stage of the company.

Having stated that, a standard business strategy will have the benchmarks listed below:

- ✓ Monthly objectives and due dates for products
- ✓ The initial two years' monthly finances
- ✓ Statements of profit and loss covering the initial three to five years
- ✓ Projections for the first three to five years' balance sheet

Business plans are written by start-ups, entrepreneurs, and small companies to serve as roadmaps for their new ventures. Bigger companies might also draft (and revise) a business plan to monitor deadlines, finances, and high-level objectives.

While a written explanation of your company's objectives and finances is undoubtedly necessary, a business plan can also assist you in assessing a company's sustainability, profitability (including the timing of its first profit), and the amount of funding you will require from investors. A company strategy, however, also serves a practical purpose: Setting goals not only helps you stay on track with your timetable but it can also draw investors and serve as a powerful growth strategy in and of itself.

5.3 Steps in Business Plan:

A business plan's particular content will change based on the requirements and objectives of your endeavour, but generally speaking, it will contain the following items in the following order:

a) Executive summary
b) Business description
c) Market analysis
d) Competitive analysis
e) Organizational management description
f) Product or service description
g) Financial predictions
h) Funding information
i) Marketing plan
j) Sales strategy

Audience, in general, consists of everyone who has a stake in one's company. They may include clients, staff members from within the company, suppliers, vendors, and both current and prospective investors.

5.4 Simple Plan vs Detailed Plan

The stage of your company and the target market determine how much depth your plan needs. A comprehensive, up to 100-page business plan is required for corporations. Start-ups and small enterprises should have a clear plan with an emphasis on strategy and finances.

5.5 How to Choose the Right Business Plan?

Asking yourself "What do we want the plan to do" will help you choose the type of business plan you need to write. Function should come first, then form. To help you decide what kind of business plan to write, refer to the chart below:

Table No. 5.1: Kind of Business Plan

Function	**Audience**	**Type of Business Plan**
Serve as a loose guide of objectives and timeline	Internal	Lean
Acts as a precise, practical roadmap for business goals and timelines.	Internal	Traditional
Serve as a strategic document with a narrative focus on organization-wide goals, priorities, and vision	Internal	Strategic
Earn a company loan or grant	External	Traditional (with focus on financial documents)
Attract investors or partners	External	Traditional/Strategic (emphasizing financials alongside support functions like marketing, sales, and product development).
To test a business or start-up idea	Internal	Lean

5.6 Is Order of the Business Plan Important?

A business plan can be written in any order, but the executive summary should always be presented first. Beyond that, just make sure the plan is arranged in a logical and organic manner.

5.7 Traditional Vs Lean Business Plans:

A traditional business plan adheres to the prescribed format; these plans typically demand more work up front and can consist of several dozen pages because they emphasize detail. Less frequently seen, a lean business plan concentrates on summarizing the most important details for every component. These blueprints are usually one page long and need a lot less labor. Generally speaking, if your organization is large, has a legacy, or doesn't follow Lean (or another Agile strategy), you should adopt a traditional model. Use Lean if you anticipate a swift pivot from the organization or if you have already implemented a Lean approach in other business processes. Additionally, if the strategy is just for internal use, a lean business plan may be adequate. Investors should stick with the traditional form since they can be more sensitive to abrupt changes or a high level of inherent flexibility in the plan.

5.8 How to write a Business Plan Step-by-Step?

Research and close attention to detail are necessary while writing a solid business plan for each part. A 10-step strategy to developing and researching each plan aspect can be found below.

- ✓ **1st Step - Executive Synopsis:** Business plan's executive summary will always come first. The purpose is to respond to the following queries:
    - o What are the company's goals and objectives?
    - o What are the short- and long-term objectives of the company?
- ✓ **2nd Step -Business Description:** The purpose of this part is to outline the nature, extent, and purpose of your endeavour. To do

this, provide as succinct and clear a response as you can to the following questions:

  - What line of work do we do?
  - What does our company do?

- ✓ **3rdStep - Analysis of the Market:** Provide proof in this part that you have studied and comprehend the market, and that your offering fills a need in the market for your product or service. To achieve this, respond to these inquiries:
  - Who is our client?
  - What is important to that client?
- ✓ **4th Step - Competitive Analysis:** A business plan frequently suggests a more competitive version of an idea rather than a completely new (or even market-disrupting) one, whether through features, pricing, integrations, etc. - greater than what is offered at this time. Provide answers to the following questions in this part to demonstrate how your good or service will surpass that of competitors:
  - Who are the rivals?
  - What skills do they possess?
  - What makes our value offer special?
- ✓ **5th Step - Describe organizational management:** Provide a brief synopsis of the team members and other important individuals who are essential to the outcome in this area. Enumerate the duties and responsibilities, and if you can, include information about the team hierarchy.
- ✓ **6thStep - Product or Service Description:** Clearly describe your product or service in this part, together with all the work and materials required to produce it. Before you start talking about marketing, sales, or funding aspects, you must take the necessary time to test and improve your product because its strength will determine your company's success to a considerable extent. The following are the questions to be answered in this section:
  - What type of product or service is it?
  - How do we make it, and what materials are needed to make it?
- ✓ **7th Step - Create a marketing strategy:** Describe your product or service's marketing plan in this section. This doesn't have to be as detailed as a comprehensive marketing plan, but it should address some fundamental issues, like the ones listed below:
  - If the target market is distinct from the current clientele, who is it?
  - How are you going to contact your intended audience?

  - What materials does your marketing plan call for, and are they available to you?
  - Could you provide an approximate timeline and budget?
  - How are you going to define success?
- ✓ **8th Step - The Sales Strategy:** Provide a summary of the sales plan that includes the objectives of each cycle, the procedures to accomplish these, and the success measures. For the sake of a business plan, this part can simply summarize the high-level goals and methods of your sales operations rather than being an extensive, detailed sales plan. Start by addressing the following questions:
  - What is the plan for selling?
  - What strategies and instruments will you employ to accomplish your objectives?
  - What possible roadblocks may you encounter, and how would you resolve them?
  - When will sales and profits start to produce a profit?
  - What success metrics exist?
- ✓ **9th Step - Funding Information**: One of the most important sections of any business plan is this one, especially if you intend to present it to investors. While a detailed financial plan is not required, you should be able to respond to the following inquiries:
  - What is your current capitalization? What is the required capital amount?
  - How will the team expand in terms of onboarding, organization, and training and development?
  - What are your physical requirements and limitations in terms of equipment, space, etc.?
- ✓ **10th Step - Financial Projections:** Investors prefer to see well-considered financial projections for the future in addition to the analysis of the fundraising efforts. As was previously mentioned, this could take one to five years, depending on the size and stage of your company. Even while these estimates won't be precise and will need to be adjusted slightly, you should be able to estimate the following:
  - When and how will the business turn a profit for the first time?
  - How will the business continue to turn a profit after that?

All of the standard components are included in this basic business plan template, including an executive summary, information on the product or service, the target market, marketing and sales tactics, etc. Once you enter your baseline data in the finance section, the template will automatically generate estimates for financial reporting, sales forecasting, and other related areas.

5.9 How to Prepare a Business Plan:

A simplified, lighter version of the larger, conventional form is a simple business plan. A basic business plan can be more than one page, unlike a one-page business plan that conveys high-level information for brief summaries (like a stakeholder presentation). The processes for writing a basic business plan are listed below, and the template also follows these procedures.

a) **Compose the Executive Summary**: This section is the same as it is in a typical business plan: it provides a summary of the company's short- and long-term goals, the prospect or main offering, and the contents of the business plan.
b) **Include a Company Overview:** Describe the overarching goal and vision of the organization.
c) **Describe the Issue and the Solution:** Clearly state the issue that your product or service is meant to address and the steps your business will take to address it. Consider this part as the opening you are trying to fill in the market.
d) **Determine the Target Market:** To whom is your business (and its offerings) intended to appeal? Try to give a quick description of your buyer personas.
e) **Write a Review of the Contest**: List the current competitors and describe your competitive advantage in this part to show that you understand the market.
f) **Give an Overview of Your Services or Products:** Put your product or service in its proper context and define it. What precisely are you offering for sale?
g) **Describe Your Marketing Tactics:** Give a brief overview of your intended marketing campaigns without going into too much detail.
h) **Include a Schedule and the Success Measures You'll Employ:** Provide a rough schedule that includes the key performance indicators (KPIs) and milestones you will use to gauge your success.
i) **Give Your Financial Projections:** Provide a summary of your financial plan that shows you have done sufficient

study and modelling. You can also enumerate the main presumptions used in the predictions.

j) **Determine Your Financing Needs:** In this stage, you will submit a request for assistance. List your suggested sources of finance together with your intended uses, taking into account everything in the business strategy.

5.10 Preparing a Business Plan for a Lean Start-up:

An Agile approach to a typical business plan is a lean start-up business plan. The plan is less concerned with precise outputs and deadlines and more with relationships, activities, and procedures (while allowing for flexibility in every area). Although a traditional and a lean business plan share some similarities, you can write a lean plan by using the procedures listed below:

a) **Include the value proposition:** When describing your good or service, keep it simple. What distinct value does your start-up want to offer clients? Verify that you can articulate the fundamental offering in plain, understandable terms and that the team is in agreement.

b) **List Your Key Partners:** Provide a list of all the companies you want to collaborate with in order to carry out your vision, including outside suppliers, partners, and vendors. This section shows that you have carefully evaluated the resources you have on hand, determined where outside help is needed, and looked into potential solutions.

c) **Highlight the Important Tasks:** Give an overview of your company's main operations, including sourcing, production, marketing, distribution routes, and client connections.

d) **List Your Essential Resources:** List the essential resources that will allow you to deliver your distinctive value, such as staff, machinery, space, and intellectual property.

e) **Identify Your Channels and Customer Relationships:** This part should detail how you plan to connect with and cultivate relationships with customers. Give a high-level overview of the entire customer experience, including the locations where you will communicate with them (online, in-store, etc.).

f) **Describe Your Channels of Marketing:** Describe the communication channels and marketing strategies you'll employ to build and maintain relationships with your clients. These include social media, email, and advertising, among others.

g) **Describe the Price Structure:** This part is very important when a business is just getting started. Which will you value more: minimizing expenses or optimizing value? Enumerate the basic start-up expenses and the steps you will take to turn a profit eventually.

h) **Disclose Your Sources of Income:** How will the business generate revenue over time? Incorporate both the direct purchase of goods or services and supplementary revenue streams like fundraisers, selling advertising space, memberships, etc.

Start-up executives may communicate the most important details from a traditional strategy by using this Lean business plan template. All of the aforementioned components are there, along with areas for a chronology, important metrics, cost structure and income sources, industry and product overviews, and more. Because the template is fully editable, you can modify it to meet the goals of your lean businesses.

5.11 Writing a Business Plan for Loan:

Many of the components of a standard business plan are included in a business plan for a loan, also known as a loan proposal, along with extra financial papers such a credit report, a loan request, and a loan payback schedule. You can also be required to submit information about stock investments, a type of collateral, and financial documents for both your company and yourself.

5.12 Key Points in Composing a Business Plan:

You have a few choices to improve your business plan in addition to including all the necessary information to give it the best possibility of obtaining funding and other resources. Take heed of these professional tips:

- ✓ **Keep things Simple:** As an adaptation of this concept, Avner Brodsky, the Co-Founder and CEO of the online marketing firm Lezgo Limited, uses the acronym KISS (keep things short and simple). He asserts, "A business plan is not a college thesis." "Just concentrate on giving the pertinent details."

- ✓ **Conduct Sufficient Research:** Business executives are advised by Michael Dean, Co-Founder of Pool Research, to "invest time in research, both internal and external (market, finance, legal etc.)." Steer clear of being overly confident or arrogant. Rather, maintain everything factual, impartial, and objective. Your plan must be self-contained, and any forecasts or assertions you make must be supported by facts. According to Brodsky, "Your business must be based on the facts of the market in the area you have selected. Obtain up-to-date information from reputable sources to ensure that the numbers have been verified by professionals.
- ✓ **Establish Specific Goals:** Ensure that your plan has specific, time-based goals. Dean emphasizes that identifying short-term goals is essential for building momentum, especially for new businesses
- ✓ **Recognize Your Weaknesses and Take Action:** "By being aware of your weaknesses, you can overcome them much more quickly than if you wait for them to appear," says Dean. Brodsky advises doing a thorough SWOT analysis to determine your weaknesses as well. "Having self-awareness will help you better define your company's mission and the strategies you will use to achieve your goals, which will benefit your business," he continues.
- ✓ **Look for Mentor or Peer Review:** Brodsky suggests, "Ask for feedback on your drafts and for areas to improve." "When your head is full of ideas for your company, sometimes an outsider can help you see what you're missing and prevent your company from becoming a whimsical endeavour."

In addition to these more useful suggestions, the language you choose is crucial and has the power to make or destroy your business plan.

5.13 Sources for Business Plan Writing

Although a template offers a wonderful overview of what should be included in a business plan, greater functionality, visibility, and real-time adjustments can be obtained with a live document or more advanced application. Software for business plans can also be used to store data, attach documents, and communicate information to stakeholders. LivePlan, Enloop, BizPlanner, PlanGuru, and iPlanner are a few well-liked choices.

5.14 Chapter Summary

Recall that the process is just as important to a successful company plan as the finished product. You'll become more aware of the business realities as you work on your plan. It will assist you in staying on course if you keep it updated. Developing and carrying out a solid small company plan can offer a step-by-step guide to achieve strategic objectives, regardless of your level of experience starting and growing multiple firms. To ensure that your small business plan is as successful as possible, think about collaborating with an outside expert rather than creating it alone.

5.15 Multiple Choice Questions

1. **Which of these is a common resource for business plan writing?**
   a) Business mentors
   b) Social media influencers
   c) Online shopping platforms
   d) Marketing agencies
   Answer: a) Business mentors
2. **Which section of the business plan outlines the company's mission and vision?**
   a) Marketing strategy
   b) Executive summary
   c) Financial projections
   d) Product description
   Answer: b) Executive summary
3. **A business plan is primarily used to:**
   a) Forecast weather conditions
   b) Secure funding and guide operations
   c) Track competitors' profits
   d) Advertise products
   Answer: b) Secure funding and guide operations

5.16 Short Type Questions

1. What are the initial steps in writing a business plan?
2. How can financial projections make a business plan more convincing?
3. Why is market research essential in the business plan process?

5.17 Essay Type Questions

1. Evaluate the benefits and limitations of using a lean business plan for start-ups.
2. Compare and contrast a simple business plan with a detailed business plan. When should each be used?
3. Discuss the financial details and projections that should be included in a business plan for loan approval.

5.18 Mini- Case Study:

Preparation of Business Plan for Small Business: A local coffee shop prepares a business plan to secure funding from a bank. The plan includes a detailed market analysis, pricing strategy, sales projections, funding requirements, and an operational plan to ensure a strong financial and operational foundation.

Question:

- What sections of the business plan were crucial for securing bank funding?
- How did the entrepreneur determine the appropriate pricing strategy for the coffee shop?
- What risk management strategies were included in the business plan?

5.19 References

1. Abrams, R. (2022). *Successful business plan: Secrets & strategies* (7th ed.). Planning Shop.
2. Shelton, H. (2014). *The secrets to writing a successful business plan*. Summit Valley Press.
3. McKeever, M. (2022). *How to write a business plan* (15th ed.). NOLO.

Chapter - 6: Marketing Management of Small Business

6.1 Introduction:

Since marketing plays a major role in an organization's performance, it is a crucial component of business. Marketing has a major impact on both production and distribution. The process of bringing a product or service to market, advertising it, and persuading consumers to make a purchase is known as marketing. Marketing, from an economic perspective, includes all activities that have to do with the formation of space, time, and possession of activities.

6.2 Definition of Marketing Management:

The process of transaction between a seller and a buyer is known as marketing. Marketing is "a human activity directed at satisfying needs and process," according to Phillip Kotler.

6.3 Importance of Marketing

Marketing begins with the consumer's unique need being identified and concludes with that need being met. The consumer is present throughout the entire marketing process, not only at the start. Meeting societal needs and desires is the aim of all corporate endeavours. Thus, the centre of attention for any business activity is marketing. Purchases and production are meaningless unless a company can effectively sell its products. When looking at it from a national perspective—which is covered below—marketing is equally significant.

- ✓ Individual and societal wants are met by means of marketing.
- ✓ By offering a large range of products and services, marketing contributes to raising people's standards of life.
- ✓ Marketing facilitates exports and creates jobs.
- ✓ Marketing assists in gathering data on customers, rivals, pricing, manufacturing, advertising, and sales rules.
- ✓ The most efficient development engine is marketing. It is the catalyst for small business creation because it releases dormant economic vitality.

6.4 Small Business Marketing: What Is It?

The goal of small business marketing is to expose potential clients or customers. Contacting these customers, who make up your target market, is crucial if you want to concentrate on meeting their unique needs and desires. This is due to the fact that 66% of consumers think businesses should be aware of their particular requirements and expectations. You can reach people who need and want your service or product using a range of paid and organic marketing strategies. You must make sure that customers can discover you whether you run a hybrid business, possess a physical store, or are solely online.

6.5 Marketing Functions: What Are They?

The seven key functions of marketing include marketing information management, finance, product and service management, pricing, promotion, selling, and distribution. Each department must collaborate to create a successful marketing strategy in order to support the expansion of your company. You may be asking yourself why it's important to comprehend every aspect of marketing. You may also be attempting to figure out how they all relate to marketing; after all, don't some of them fall under the purview of other teams? Collaboration amongst all teams is necessary for functional marketing to succeed.Every marketing function influences the others, therefore success demands an integrated approach. For example, the success of your sales staff is impacted by your marketing communications, and the effectiveness of your promotions is determined by your distribution plan. You'll discover how they all interact to give your marketing strategy more depth as we examine each marketing function in detail.

6.6 Seven Ways Small Business Marketing Can Be Used

Are you prepared to delve further into the roles that marketing plays and how to include them into your plan? For a summary of each, continue reading!

1. **Management of Marketing Information**: Robust data is essential for functional marketing. Data pertinent to your

marketing processes are methodically gathered and reported on via marketing information management. This data consists of:

- ✓ **Determining Your Target Market**: Identifying a specific customer group that aligns with your product/service and goals.
- ✓ **Understanding Your Target Market**: Gaining deep insights into the target market's needs, wants, and goals to create a resonant marketing strategy.
- ✓ **SWOT Analysis**: Assessing your business's internal strengths and weaknesses and external opportunities and threats. Also, consider factors like regulations and cultural trends.
- ✓ **Analysing Competitors**: Understanding what competitors do well and where they fall short to differentiate your business strategically.

2. **Financing**:
   - ✓ Businesses need to secure funds for both operations and ongoing marketing efforts.
   - ✓ Use data from past campaigns and key performance indicators (KPIs) to demonstrate the ROI of your marketing strategies and secure continued funding.
3. **Product and Service Management**:
   - ✓ The product/service is central to all marketing efforts.
   - ✓ Collaboration with the research and development team is crucial to ensure the product meets the target audience's needs.
   - ✓ Pre-launch and post-launch marketing research are important for understanding how well the product resonates with customers and for informing future updates.
4. **Pricing**:
   - ✓ Pricing is influenced by factors such as product quality, benefits, branding, customer experience, and competitive landscape.
   - ✓ The price should reflect the value of the offering and align with the target market's perceptions and business goals.
5. **Promotion**:
   - ✓ Promotion involves all communication strategies to make the target audience aware of the product.

- ✓ Use a mix of channels (websites, SEO, social media, etc.) based on your target audience, competitive landscape, and marketing goals.
- ✓ Effective promotion encourages two-way communication and builds strong brand-customer relationships.

6. **Selling**:
   - ✓ Selling is a key marketing function, involving guiding potential customers through the buyer's journey towards a purchase.
   - ✓ Use various communication channels and content to nurture leads through awareness, consideration, and decision stages.

7. **Distribution**:
   - ✓ Distribution involves getting the product to the buyers through channels like E-Commerce stores, in-person stores, wholesalers, etc.
   - ✓ The distribution strategy must align with marketing efforts to ensure customers receive the product after being persuaded to purchase.

This comprehensive overview covers the essential elements needed to develop a successful marketing strategy, from understanding your target market to securing financing, managing your product, setting the right price, promoting effectively, closing sales, and ensuring efficient distribution.

6.7 Essentials of Small Business Marketing: Tools and Technology

The tools and technology you choose for your small business marketing depend on your company's size and needs. While some tools are essential, others may simply enhance your marketing efforts. Regardless, the following tools are highly recommended to help you get started.

- ✓ **CRM Platform:** A Customer Relationship Management (CRM) system is crucial for organizing both prospective and existing customer data in a single location. This centralized data, coupled with effective record-keeping, is invaluable for your sales, marketing, and customer success teams. A CRM platform enables you to uncover actionable insights, monitor customer interactions, and manage the entire customer journey, allowing you to better tailor your marketing campaigns. Notably, half of small and midsize businesses in the U.S. use a CRM system, with 15% having implemented it within the past year.

✓ **Digital Marketing Platforms:** These platforms typically offer a blend of features like organization, automation, and tracking of various marketing activities. Many of these tools can integrate with your CRM platform. Here are some specialized types of digital marketing platforms:
   - **Email Marketing Platform:** This software enables the creation and design of email campaigns. You can store email addresses of leads and customers, segment your audience, and send targeted messages based on where prospects are in the purchase funnel. Additionally, it allows you to track user behavior, such as open rates, click-through rates, and links clicked.
   - **SMS Marketing Platform:** This service can function as a standalone tool or be integrated into a larger email marketing platform. SMS marketing, or text messaging, is an effective way to reach customers, considering how many people have smartphones on hand. Businesses can use SMS to communicate flash deals, new products, and more to customers who opt in to receive these messages.
   - **Social Media Marketing Platform:** Marketers use this software to manage social media activities, engage with their audience, grow followers, and schedule posts. It also provides valuable insights and metrics about the audience, which can inform decisions on what and when to post. Additionally, social media listening tools allow businesses to monitor industry and brand-related conversations, enabling them to engage with users.
   - **Influencer Marketing Platform:** This newer type of platform assists businesses in creating influencer marketing campaigns. It helps marketers identify both niche and general social media and video influencers, set up campaigns, and track return on investment (ROI).

6.8 Market Research Tools for Small Businesses

Conducting market research is essential for small businesses, and it doesn't have to be expensive. Before investing heavily in any marketing effort, it's important to research everything, from your ideal customer profile to the competitive landscape. Start by setting a budget, deciding on the data you need, and choosing how to gather that information.

- ✓ **Google Analytics:** Google Analytics is a powerful tool that tracks various data about website visitors and generates reports to help marketers make informed decisions about their website's effectiveness. It allows you to analyse visitor demographics, locations, age groups, and even the devices they use to access your site. Additionally, it provides insights into which pages and content on your site are the most popular, how long visitors stay on your site, conversion rates, and more. In essence, Google Analytics offers a wealth of data that SEO specialists can use to derive actionable insights.
- ✓ **Steps to Begin Using Google Analytics:**
    - Create a Google Analytics account.
    - Set up the property you wish to track, such as your business website.
    - Insert the tracking code into your website.

  Once the account is properly set up, it typically takes 24 to 48 hours to start seeing data in your Google Analytics account. This tool is crucial, as nearly all marketers will be using their company website to reach prospects and customers over the next year.
- ✓ **Content Calendar:** A content calendar serves as a centralized location where you schedule and organize all of your company's content. This can include blog posts, YouTube videos, social media updates, and any other marketing materials your company plans to publish during a specific time period. You can use a shared online calendar or a spreadsheet with monthly tabs alongside project management software to keep track of each piece of content. The calendar helps you manage tasks from initial production to promotion, assign responsibilities to team members, and track deadlines.
- ✓ **Example Workflow for a Blog Post:**
    - Add the blog post title to the target publish date on the company-wide calendar.
    - Create a project for the blog post in your project management software.

- Break down the project into individual tasks (e.g., write the blog post, source images, prepare social media copy) with corresponding deadlines.
- Assign each task to the responsible team member, such as the writer, editor, graphic designer, SEO specialist, or social media manager.
- Mark tasks as completed or use a color-coded system to track progress.

Regular communication with your team is essential to ensure content stays on track and meets deadlines. Be open to adjusting your process as needed. For small or lean content teams, an online calendar with publishing dates might suffice in the early stages. Depending on your industry, you may need to schedule content anywhere from one to six months in advance, allowing for flexibility in case of delays or changes. For example, if you're planning a major Black Friday promotion, start planning and creating content months before November.

6.9 A Summary of Marketing Channels and Activities

Small business owners should recognize the array of marketing opportunities available, even if they don't utilize them right away. Here's an overview of key marketing tools across different content and activity types.

1. **Readable Content:**
   - **Articles:** These are well-researched pieces that include original data, facts, and expert insights, sometimes incorporating interviews or written by industry specialists.
   - **Blog Posts:** Similar to articles but often more opinionated, blog posts typically focus on a company's products and services, offering a direct voice to the business.
   - **E-books:** Longer than articles or blog posts, e-books usually aim for 2,000+ words and provide in-depth content with original research. They are digital products and are often gated, requiring payment or an email address for access.

- **White Papers:** Authoritative and research-intensive, white papers are similar to e-books and are also often gated. They delve deeply into specific topics or industry trends.
- **Landing Pages:** These are targeted pages on a website designed to prompt visitors to take specific actions, such as signing up for a service or making a purchase. Often used in conjunction with specific marketing campaigns.

2. **Visuals and Visual Content:**
   - **Infographics:** Visual representations of data or research, often with original artwork. Including your logo and embedding HTML allows others to share it, helping to generate backlinks.
   - **Photos:** Whether product images or user-generated content, photos are key to grabbing attention. These can be repurposed across email and social media, with editing tools enhancing their appearance.
   - **Videos:** Depending on the type, videos can be shot with a smartphone or produced professionally. They might showcase behind-the-scenes footage or demonstrate how a product works.
   - **Webinars:** Also called video conferences, webinars allow businesses to reach and inform multiple audiences at once, often accompanied by special promotions for attendees.
   - **Podcasts:** These audio episodes can be downloaded or streamed, ranging from short to long-form, and often feature expert guests discussing niche or broad topics.
3. **Online Marketing Activities:**
   - **Search Engine Optimization (SEO):** A crucial strategy for being found online. Whether done in-house or with an external expert, SEO helps increase your visibility on search engines.
   - **Google My Business:** A free tool that allows businesses to manage their online presence, including location, hours, photos, and customer reviews.

- **Remarketing and Retargeting:** Both involve reaching out to potential customers based on their online behavior. Remarketing often involves email reminders, while retargeting displays ads to users who have previously visited your site.
- **Email Marketing:** A highly effective channel for engaging with customers, offering a great ROI. A strong email strategy allows you to tailor content to different customer segments, boosting sales.
- **Social Media Marketing:** A popular method for connecting with customers, promoting products, and expanding market presence through organic and paid posts.
- **Influencer Marketing:** Collaborating with influencers, even those with small followings, can help promote your business to their engaged audiences in exchange for compensation, free products, or a share of sales.
- **Search Engine Marketing (SEM):** An advertising strategy that increases visibility on search engine results pages (SERPs) through paid ads. Pay-per-click (PPC) ads, where businesses pay per click, can help companies stand out and compete, especially during the discovery phase.

4. **Offline Marketing Activities**
    - **Direct Mail:** This involves sending physical advertisements, like postcards, coupon booklets, or catalogues, directly to homes or businesses to promote your company.
    - **In-Person Events:** Hosting or sponsoring events, whether at a conference or a local venue, can generate business and build connections. For tips on event marketing, Salesforce's e-book "Getting Started with Small Business Marketing" can be helpful.
    - **Retail Spaces:** Small businesses that sell both online and in brick-and-mortar stores can use both channels to draw in customers and boost sales. Gathering customer data through in-

person surveys and kiosks can provide valuable insights. Tools like Salesforce's Retail CRM can help organize customer information and deliver personalized shopping experiences.

5. **Relationship-Building Marketing Activities**
    - **Business Associations:** These organizations, also known as trade associations, unite business owners within a particular industry and offer resources and support, often with membership perks like discounts on education or insurance.
    - **Chamber of Commerce:** This local business organization works to promote the business community, offering resources, events, and other membership benefits similar to business associations.
    - **Rotary Club:** An international organization that brings together business and professional leaders to engage in humanitarian efforts.

These are just a few ways to connect with your audience. Small businesses have numerous opportunities for networking and promoting goodwill, including charities and sponsorships. Use data, experiment with different strategies, and find the right marketing mix for your business.

6.10 Handling Your Marketing: In-House, Consultant, or Agency?

When deciding how to manage your marketing, consider these questions:

- ✓ Define my goals?
- ✓ Plan my budget?
- ✓ What are my areas of weakness or lack of expertise?

Depending on your answers, you might choose to keep marketing in-house, hire a consultant, or work with an agency. If your company is growing quickly or needs external expertise, it may be wise to hire a specialist or agency. If you don't yet have a marketing budget, now is the time to create one and align it with your strategy to determine who you can afford to hire. In both B2C and B2B companies, advertising typically represents the largest portion of the marketing budget, followed closely by technology investments. Whether your budget is limited or expansive, you can still effectively reach your leads and customers.

6.11 Competitive Advantage of Small Business Management: Strategies for Competing with Big Brands

Small businesses face competition not only from other local businesses but also from large brands with substantial marketing budgets and brand recognition. However, small businesses have unique advantages:

1. **Establish a Strong Digital Presence:** Digital marketing enables small businesses to create a significant online presence with minimal investment. Organic social media marketing and targeted digital ads can reach new audiences cost-effectively, while traditional methods like print ads and direct mail can be optimized using modern data and analytics.
2. **Test Marketing Trends:** Small businesses can be more agile than large corporations, allowing them to quickly test and adapt to new marketing trends. With fewer bureaucratic hurdles, small businesses can innovate and respond to market changes faster.
3. **Build a Strong Reputation:** A small business can cultivate a strong local reputation, which can be more impactful than a large but impersonal corporate presence. Focusing on customer feedback and online reviews can help build and maintain this reputation.
4. **Deliver Exceptional Customer Service:** Small businesses can offer personalized customer service, creating deeper relationships with customers. This level of service can be a significant competitive advantage over larger companies.
5. **Implement Customer Feedback:** Small businesses can quickly act on customer feedback to improve their offerings and enhance customer experience, something that large corporations may struggle to do as efficiently.
6. **Segment and Refine Your Audience:** Small businesses can effectively target specific local demographics, using their understanding of the community to tailor their marketing efforts. Utilizing tools like Facebook's lookalike audience targeting can further enhance this strategy.

7. **Leverage Branded Content:** Creative and engaging branded content can help a small business stand out in the local market. By aligning content with customer values and using the right digital channels, small businesses can enhance their brand presence.
8. **Enhance Design:** Professional design elements like logos, websites, and social media assets are crucial for competing with larger brands. Collaborating with skilled designers can elevate a small business's online and offline presence.
9. **Create a Customer Loyalty Program:** Offering a customer loyalty program can encourage repeat business and emphasize the local, community-focused aspect of the business.
10. **Get involved in the Community:** Small businesses can build stronger connections with their community through local involvement, such as donations, volunteering, and personal interactions with customers.
11. **Run Local Promotions and Contests:** Small businesses can easily create and manage local promotions and contests, which can drive customer engagement and attract more business.
12. **Attract Top Talent:** Building a positive workplace culture and offering unique perks can help small businesses attract and retain top talent, contributing to better customer service and overall business success.

6.12 Don't Let Big Brands Overshadow Your Business

Operating a small business in a local market means you're competing with nearby national chains. However, this doesn’t mean your business will be overshadowed. With clever marketing and by leveraging your local status, you can thrive even alongside larger competitors. Here are 12 strategies to help small businesses stand out against big brands:

- ✓ Build a Strong Digital Footprint
- ✓ Experiment with Marketing Trends
- ✓ Enhance Your Business's Reputation
- ✓ Provide Exceptional Customer Service
- ✓ Implement Feedback for Continuous Improvement

- ✓ Focus on Specific Target Audiences
- ✓ Utilize Localized Branded Content
- ✓ Improve Your Design Aesthetic
- ✓ Develop a Customer Loyalty Program
- ✓ Engage with the Community
- ✓ Offer Local Promotions & Contests
- ✓ Recruit Top Talent

6.13 Sales Strategies for Business Growth: How to Develop a Sales Strategy to Increase Small Business Sales?

Every business, knowingly or unknowingly, operates with a sales strategy. This isn't something exclusive to large companies. Every founder has pondered over:

- ✓ The most effective way to market and sell their product or service.
- ✓ How to ensure its success.

In essence, that's what a sales strategy is all about, and we'll explore how it can significantly boost your small business sales.

What is a Sales Strategy? A sales strategy is a carefully devised plan to sell a product or service in the market, aiming to maximize profitability. A good sales strategy prioritizes the value proposition from the customer's point of view. It's not just something you establish when launching a new product; it's a dynamic plan continuously refined by key players like the Sales Head, Sales Manager, and CEO.

Why Small Businesses Need a Robust Sales Strategy: Given that consumer behaviour is unpredictable, strategies often deviate from the plan. The key to a successful strategy is starting with a solid foundation and continuously refining it based on customer feedback and brand performance. For small businesses, a well-crafted sales strategy is crucial for optimizing resources and time.

Preparing for a Successful Sales Strategy: To build a successful sales strategy, start with a strong foundation that includes:

- ✓ **Deep Customer Understanding**: Truly knowing your target audience goes beyond just demographics. It's about understanding their aspirations, pain points, and what drives their buying decisions. Creating buyer personas can help you target your audience more effectively.

- ✓ **Market Knowledge**: Whether launching a new product or selling an existing one, understanding the market landscape is essential. This includes knowing how the market has reacted to similar products, understanding competitor dynamics, and staying updated on market changes.
- ✓ **Thorough Product Knowledge**: Fully grasping the nuances of your product, including its unique value proposition, is critical. This deep understanding will empower your sales team to make compelling pitches.
- ✓ **Competitor Awareness**: Understanding both direct and indirect competitors is vital. Analysing their sales strategies can help you differentiate your offering and avoid replicating what others are doing.

Diverse Sales Strategies to Boost Small Business Sales: When creating a sales strategy, you can choose from various approaches, techniques, and practices. Here's a detailed look at each:

a) Sales Approaches:

- **Demand Generation**: A proactive approach where the sales team generates qualified leads, streamlining the lead qualification process and saving time.
- **Content Marketing**: Ensuring your business is visible to customers throughout their buying journey by utilizing various content channels.
- **Referral Sales**: Leveraging satisfied customers and prospects to refer others who could benefit from your product, thus speeding up the sales process.
- **Account-Based Sales**: Ideal for B2B businesses, this approach involves targeting specific companies and tailoring pitches to individual stakeholders.

b) **Sales Techniques**:

- **Selling Solutions, Not Just Products**: Focusing on how your product solves a problem for the customer, rather than just listing features.

- **Start and End Strong**: Capturing interest early in the conversation and confidently closing by asking for the sale.
- **Targeting Urgent Needs**: Prioritizing prospects who have an immediate need for your product or service.
- **Active Listening**: Using cues from prospects to tailor your pitch and keep them engaged.

c) **Sales Practices**:

- **Utilizing Technology**: Leveraging tools like CRM software to manage leads, streamline communication, and optimize sales processes.
- **Lead Nurturing**: Keeping prospects engaged through regular communication until they are ready to make a purchase.
- **Upselling**: Offering existing customers upgraded versions or additional features of a product they already use.
- **Cross-Selling**: Introducing customers to related products that complement their existing purchases.

6.14 Marketing Strategies for Small Businesses

Marketing plays a crucial role in the success of small businesses, helping to attract customers and achieve sales goals. Here are eight effective marketing strategies to set your business on the path to success:

✓ **Build a Brand**: Establish a clear brand identity with a consistent logo, color scheme, and imagery that communicates your company's values and offerings.

✓ **Understand Your Customer**: Develop a marketing strategy tailored to your specific audience by understanding their demographics, preferences, and online behaviors.

✓ **Create a website**: Your website is the cornerstone of your marketing strategy, serving as a digital business card and a hub for customer interaction.

✓ **Leverage SEO**: Optimize your website with relevant keywords to rank higher on Google and attract more organic traffic.

- ✓ **Get Listed on Google**: Utilize Google My Business to enhance your visibility in local searches and build credibility with potential customers.
- ✓ **Advertise on Facebook**: Use Facebook Ads to target specific demographics and reach a large audience quickly and cost-effectively.
- ✓ **Email Marketing**: Engage with customers and prospects through personalized and relevant email campaigns that keep your brand top-of-mind.
- ✓ **Use Google AdWords**: Invest in Google AdWords to increase your visibility in search results and drive more traffic to your website.

6.15 Chapter Summary

Effective management of small businesses is key to achieving success and growth. By focusing on clear business planning, exceptional customer experiences, digital marketing, and sound financial management, small businesses can thrive. Embracing technology, building a strong team, and staying adaptable to market changes are also critical. Prioritizing customer retention and monitoring key performance indicators will further enhance your business's performance. Marketing should be a dynamic process, constantly evolving with your business and customer needs. By investing in creative, data-driven marketing strategies, you can achieve significant growth and reach your business goals.

6.16 Multiple Choice Questions

1. Which strategy helps small businesses stand out against big brands?
   a) Ignoring branding efforts
   b) Focusing on niche markets
   c) Offering standardized products
   d) Avoiding social media presence
   Answer: b) Focusing on niche markets
2. Which tool is commonly used for small business market research?
   a) Google Analytics
   b) Cash flow software
   c) HR management systems

d) Cloud storage
Answer: a) Google Analytics

3. Why is marketing important for small businesses?
   a) To create brand awareness and attract customers
   b) To reduce operational costs
   c) To ensure financial stability
   d) To avoid competition
   Answer: a) To create brand awareness and attract customers

6.17 Short Type Questions

1. How can small businesses leverage social media for effective marketing?
2. When should a small business consider hiring a consultant or agency for marketing?
3. What is the role of marketing in small business management?

6.18 Essay Type Questions

1. Outline the key marketing functions and their relevance to small businesses.
2. Enumerate the unique challenges and opportunities small businesses face in marketing.
3. Discuss how marketing strategies differ for small businesses compared to large corporations.

6.19 Mini- Case Study: Marketing

Management of Small Business: A new handmade jewellery business uses social media marketing to build brand awareness. The case examines how the entrepreneur creates effective online campaigns, utilizes customer feedback, and adjusts strategies to increase sales.

Question:

- What role did social media marketing play in the success of the handmade jewellery business?
- How did the entrepreneur utilize customer feedback to refine the marketing strategy?
- What are some ways the business can improve its digital marketing efforts?

6.20 References

1. Aaker, D. A., & Shansby, J. G. (2016). *Marketing for small businesses: An essential guide*. CreateSpace Independent Publishing.
2. Kotler, P., Armstrong, G., Harris, L. C., & Piercy, N. (2020). *Principles of marketing* (8th European ed.). Pearson.
3. Kotler, P., & Keller, K. L. (2022). *Marketing management* (16th ed.). Pearson.

Chapter - 7: Human Resource Management in Small Business

7.1 Introduction

Effectively managing the recruitment, training, and compensation of employees is crucial for the success of any small business. Typically, small businesses employ fewer than a hundred individuals, a number that, while modest, requires professional human resource management to streamline HR functions. Human resource management encompasses both the physical and mental contributions of the workforce in producing goods and services for the company. Research indicates that in small businesses, functions like finance, accounting, and marketing often take precedence over human resources. As a result, many small businesses lack full-time HR managers to oversee all aspects of human resource management. Small business owners face unique challenges in this area, but with the right strategies and resources, they can establish an effective HR system that contributes to the success of their business. Implementing sound HR practices can give your business a competitive edge.

7.2 Investing in HR for Business Growth

Small businesses often prioritize marketing and sales strategies to expand their customer base, and they may invest in advanced technology to improve efficiency, such as subscribing to a marketing platform that uses AI and machine learning for data capture and customer analysis. Other operational areas, including financial management and product or service development, also benefit from such investments. However, human resource management often receives less attention. The delay in investing in HR management can be attributed to several factors, including a do-it-yourself mentality common in small businesses, a primary focus on sales strategies, and a lack of confidence that HR investments will yield tangible results. Nonetheless, forward-thinking businesses recognize the value of investing in HR management, including HR management software, to drive innovation, productivity, efficiency, and employee morale.

7.3 Understanding Human Resources

Human resources (HR) is a department responsible for managing employee relations within a company. HR professionals handle various aspects of an employee's lifecycle, including recruitment, on-boarding, payroll processing, benefits management, performance reviews, and conducting exit interviews. Additionally, HR ensures compliance with labor laws, promotes company policies, and acts as a mediator between employers and employees.

7.4 Why Invest in HR Management?

Employees are a business's most valuable asset, and investing in their development can lead to higher retention rates, an improved workplace culture, and increased productivity and sales. Other reasons to invest in HR management include attracting top talent, reducing employee turnover, building a strong brand, and creating a competitive advantage. While investing in HR management may not always be glamorous, it is a critical strategy for ensuring the long-term survival and success of your business.

7.5 Objectives of Human Resource Management

The primary objectives of human resource management (HRM) are to create a seamless experience for employees and other stakeholders while achieving organizational goals. These objectives include ensuring the availability of resources, providing easy access to data, processing payroll on time, and maintaining compliance with regulations. HRM objectives are closely aligned with the overall goals of the organization, aimed at enhancing productivity and profitability. Key objectives of HRM include: a) Achieving organizational goals b) Fostering a positive work culture c) Integrating teams d) Providing training and development opportunities e) Motivating employees f) Empowering the workforce g) Retaining talent h) Managing data and ensuring compliance

7.6 The Importance of Having an HR Department

A HR department is essential for maintaining a harmonious relationship between a company and its employees. HR ensures compliance with labor laws that create satisfactory working conditions and serves as a mediator between management and staff, facilitating the exchange of ideas and concerns. Having at least one HR professional in your business can save you time by handling recruitment, hiring, on-boarding, and paperwork, allowing you to focus on growing your business.

7.7 Four Key Functions of HR

HR departments play a critical role in ensuring that a business operates smoothly. The four key functions of HR are business development, employee advocacy, change implementation, and managing salary and benefits.

1. **Business Development**: HR is responsible for staffing and on-boarding, which includes reviewing the employee handbook, completing necessary paperwork, and providing training. HR also develops business plans that align with company objectives

and ensures systems run smoothly. If employees are not adhering to company protocols, HR may send communications or lead presentations to reinforce expectations. Additionally, HR creates employee engagement initiatives, such as team-building activities.

2. **Employee Advocacy**: HR professionals provide support and guidance to employees, promoting their best interests while ensuring that the company complies with labor and human rights laws. They ensure that all employees, including management, follow company policies and act appropriately. Employees can contact HR with questions about policies, benefits, or protocols and share concerns or suggestions.
3. **Change Implementation**: The HR department communicates organizational or policy changes to employees. HR managers review company operations to identify solutions that benefit both the business and its employees. Changes may include implementing new systems, updating policies, or introducing new benefits. HR often acts as a bridge between employees and management, finding compromises that ensure business success and employee satisfaction.
4. **Salary and Benefits**: HR handles payroll processing and manages employee benefits, such as paid time off, retirement plans, and health insurance. HR professionals research competitive compensation and negotiate salaries and benefits during the hiring process. They also manage compensation adjustments, vacation, and sick leave.

7.8 Different Roles in HR:

HR encompasses various roles, each focusing on specific functions:

- ✓ **Human Resources Generalist**: Manages day-to-day HR activities and has knowledge across most HR functions.

- ✓ **Compensation and Benefits Specialist**: Focuses on employee pay and benefits, handling raises, promotions, and communicating benefit changes.
- ✓ **Development Specialist**: Helps train and develop employees, aiding their growth within the company.
- ✓ **Employee Relations Specialist**: Works to foster positive relationships between employees, managers, and employers.
- ✓ **Human Resources Representative**: Handles a wide range of HR tasks, making them valuable for smaller companies.
- ✓ **Human Resources Manager**: Oversees HR staff, updates policies, and develops new employee development plans.

7.9 Managing HR in Small Business Management:

Essential Tips for Small Business Owners Owning a small business requires juggling many responsibilities, from strategic decision-making to day-to-day operations like closing sales, negotiating with vendors, and managing finances. As a result, HR management may take a backseat, but neglecting HR can lead to costly legal issues and lost productivity. Understanding and managing HR effectively can bring significant benefits, including attracting and retaining a talented workforce. Below are essential HR tips for small business owners:

1. **Hire the Best People**: Effective HR management starts with hiring the right people. Take your time during the recruitment process, clearly defining the role and required qualifications. Prepare thoroughly for interviews, asking questions that reveal the candidate's goals and suitability for the position.
2. **Offer Competitive Compensation Packages**: To attract top talent, offer competitive pay and benefits. Research what other companies offer and provide benefits that a small business can uniquely offer, such as flexible personal and sick leave policies.
3. **Get the On-boarding Process Right**: Ensure new employees are productive quickly by having a well-

prepared on-boarding process. Introduce them to the team, explain the company's operations, and provide training to help them settle into their role.

4. **Familiarize Yourself with Employment Law**: Understand the employment laws and regulations that apply to your region. Hiring an employment law expert can help protect your business and employees.
5. **Run Your Payroll Efficiently**: Timely and accurate payroll processing is critical for maintaining employee trust. Consider using payroll software or hiring a qualified person to handle payroll.
6. **Establish Clear Employment Policies**: Create an employee handbook that outlines your company's employment policies, including pay, benefits, termination procedures, and safety guidelines.
7. **Provide Opportunities for Employee Growth**: Offer training and development opportunities to retain top talent and support employee growth within your company.
8. **Communicate Clearly with Employees**: Maintain open communication with your employees, keeping them informed about company developments and encouraging feedback.
9. **Create a Safe Work Environment**: Ensure compliance with safety regulations and prepare for potential emergencies. A secure work environment is essential for ensuring employee well-being.
10. **Happy Employees are Productive Employees**: Beyond legal compliance, HR is about building a positive relationship with your workforce. A satisfied workforce is more productive and contributes to the long-term success of your business.

7.10 Key HR Strategies for Small Businesses

Explore essential strategies for human resource management in small businesses, including recruitment, staff management, on-boarding, rewards, and training plans:

1. **Establish a Standardized Recruitment Process**: Create a clear recruitment process that defines the roles, qualifications, and experience required for each position. Publicize these requirements and develop an assessment plan to evaluate candidates.

2. **Recruitment and Management of Staff and Freelancers**: Decide whether to hire permanent staff or outsource tasks to contractors. As your business grows, assess the best approach for your company's needs.
3. **Ensure an Effective On-boarding and Orientation Program**: Develop a plan to quickly integrate new hires into your team, ensuring they understand their roles and company policies.
4. **Develop Clear Job Descriptions for Each Role**: Document job descriptions to clarify roles and responsibilities, helping to reduce miscommunication and set performance expectations.
5. **Keep Accurate Records of Employee Benefits and Compensation**: Regularly update records to ensure employees receive correct benefits and wages, protecting your business from potential disputes.
6. **Develop Ongoing Training Plans for Employees**: Invest in employee development by creating training plans that support individual growth and contribute to your business's success.
7. **Adopt Best Practices to Retain Talent**: Stay competitive by adopting industry best practices to keep employees satisfied and engaged.
8. **Rewards and Remuneration**: Develop fair and consistent compensation packages, considering factors like years of service and benefits, to avoid discontent among employees.

7.11 Chapter Summary

Implementing an effective human resource management system is crucial for the growth and competitiveness of small businesses. By investing in HR systems, companies can motivate employees, foster a positive work environment, and build a strong brand. Establishing a solid HR framework may involve significant effort and investment, but the long-term benefits of a satisfied, productive workforce far outweigh the costs.

7.12 Multiple Choice Questions

1. What does HRM stand for?
   a) Human Resource Management

b) Human Recruitment Management
c) Human Relation Management
d) Human Rights Management
Answer: a) Human Resource Management

2. What is the primary role of HR in a business?
a) Managing financial accounts
b) Managing and developing the workforce
c) Designing marketing strategies
d) Increasing production output
Answer: b) Managing and developing the workforce
3. What is a key HR strategy for small businesses?
a) Offering flexible work schedules
b) Ignoring training programs
c) Reducing wages to cut costs
d) Avoiding performance evaluations
Answer: a) Offering flexible work schedules

7.13 Short Type Questions

1. Mention two key benefits of investing in HR for small businesses.
2. Define the term "Human Resources" in a business context.
3. How can an HR department improve employee retention?

7.14 Essay Type Questions

1. Evaluate the challenges small businesses face when investing in HR resources.
2. Outline the primary objectives of HRM and their relevance to small businesses.
3. Compare the roles of HR specialists and HR generalists in small business environments.

7.15 Mini- Case Study

A family-owned restaurant hires its first full-time employee. The case covers the challenges of managing staff, including hiring, training, conflict resolution, and ensuring legal compliance with labor laws in a small business environment.

Question:

- How did the family-owned restaurant approach hiring and training its first full-time employee?

- What challenges did the restaurant face in managing employee expectations and maintaining team dynamics?
- How can the restaurant ensure compliance with labor laws while still maintaining a family-like atmosphere?

7.16 References

1. Dessler, G. (2020). *Human resource management* (16th ed.). Pearson Education.
2. Mathis, R. L., Jackson, J. H., Valentine, S. R., & Meglich, P. A. (2023). *Human resource management* (16th ed.). Cengage Learning.
3. Baron, J. N., & Kreps, D. M. (1999). *Strategic human resources: Frameworks for general managers*. Wiley.

Chapter - 8: Financing Planning in Small Business

8.1 Introduction
8.2 Why Are Budgeting and Financial Planning Crucial for Small Businesses?
8.3 Creating a Business Budget for Efficient Resource Allocation
8.4 How to Manage Your Finances and Stick to Your Budget
8.5 Common Mistakes Small Businesses Make When Budgeting and Planning Their Finances
8.6 Financial Planning Techniques for Business Growth
8.7 Tips and Tricks for Staying on Budget
8.8 The Financial Planning Process
8.9 Budgeting and financial planning
8.10 Four Steps to Develop a Financial Plan for Your Small Business
8.11 Chapter Summary
8.12 Multiple choice questions
8.13 Short type questions
8.14 Essay type questions
8.15 Mini- Case Study
8.16 References

8.1 Introduction

A robust financial strategy is essential for success, whether you're launching a new venture or looking to grow an existing one. Budgeting is key to effectively managing resources, tracking your finances, and making informed decisions that drive growth. However, managing finances is often one of the less enjoyable aspects of running a business. That's where we come in. At Protea Financial, our team of experienced bookkeepers is here to help you navigate the complexities of budgeting and financial planning, allowing you to focus on what you do best: building your business. So, sit back and let us guide you through the essentials of company budgeting and financial planning. Trust us; this journey will be enlightening and help propel your business to new heights!

8.2 Why Are Budgeting and Financial Planning Crucial for Small Businesses?

- ✓ Budgeting and financial planning are fundamental to the success of small businesses. With limited resources, it's crucial to use them wisely to maximize efficiency and growth.
- ✓ Budgeting provides business owners with a clear view of their financial health. By tracking income and expenses, they can identify areas where costs can be reduced or revenue can be increased, leading to informed decision-making and avoiding unnecessary spending.
- ✓ A well-crafted budget also enables small businesses to set realistic goals and objectives. It serves as a roadmap for achieving those goals by outlining the necessary steps and allocating funds accordingly.
- ✓ Financial planning is vital for managing cash flow effectively. By forecasting future expenses and income streams, businesses can ensure they have enough liquidity to meet operational needs without facing cash shortages.
- ✓ Budgeting also promotes accountability within the organization. When employees understand the company's financial constraints, they are more likely to make cost-effective decisions in their roles.

- ✓ Budgeting and financial planning play a key role in risk management. Small businesses often face uncertainties such as economic fluctuations or unexpected expenses. A solid financial strategy helps anticipate potential risks and develop appropriate mitigation strategies.
- ✓ Budgeting goes beyond merely tracking finances; it is an essential tool for the survival and success of small businesses. It offers valuable insights into operations, guides resource allocation, and informs decision-making processes.

8.3 Creating a Business Budget for Efficient Resource Allocation

- ✓ One of the most critical aspects of managing a small business is creating a budget that enables optimal resource allocation. Proper planning and allocation of funds ensure that your business operates smoothly and efficiently.
- ✓ Start by assessing your company's current financial situation. Take inventory of all revenue and expense sources, including fixed costs like rent or utilities, variable costs such as inventory or marketing expenses, and any outstanding debts or loans. This will provide you with a clear view of how your money is being allocated.
- ✓ Next, set clear financial goals for your business. Do you want to increase revenue? Reduce costs? Expand into new markets? Clearly defined goals will guide your budget decisions and help allocate resources appropriately.
- ✓ Once your goals are set, create a detailed budget outlining projected income and expenses over a specific period. Include both short-term (monthly) and long-term (quarterly or yearly) budgets to account for cash flow fluctuations.
- ✓ It's important to be realistic about projected revenue and expenses when creating your budget. Consider market trends, competition, seasonality, and other factors that could impact your finances.
- ✓ Regularly monitor and evaluate your budget to ensure its accuracy and make necessary adjustments. Compare

actual data with projections to identify areas where resources may need to be reallocated or cost-saving measures implemented.

- ✓ By developing an effective business budget for resource allocation, you set the stage for successfully managing your small business's financial health.

8.4 How to Manage Your Finances and Stick to Your Budget

- ✓ Keeping accurate financial records and sticking to a budget is crucial for your small business's success. It gives you a comprehensive view of your income, expenses, and overall financial health. But how do you effectively manage your finances and adhere to your budget?
- ✓ It's essential to have a system for recording all financial transactions. This could be as simple as using spreadsheets or investing in accounting software to automate the process. Be sure to categorize each transaction accurately to track where your money is going.
- ✓ Regularly reviewing and reconciling bank statements is also important. This helps identify any discrepancies in your records so that they can be addressed promptly.
- ✓ Another useful tip is to keep personal and business finances separate. Having separate bank accounts and credit cards for business expenses makes tracking easier and ensures personal spending doesn't interfere with budget accuracy.
- ✓ Monitoring cash flow is also crucial. By keeping an eye on incoming and outgoing funds, you can anticipate periods of low cash flow and take proactive steps such as adjusting payment terms with suppliers or seeking additional financing if needed.
- ✓ Consider setting aside time each week or month to review your finances. Use this time to analyze trends, identify cost-saving opportunities, and make any necessary adjustments.
- ✓ Remember, managing finances isn't just about keeping records; it's about gaining insights into your company's

financial health. Regular analysis will help you make informed decisions about investments, expansion plans, marketing strategies, and more, ultimately driving growth.

8.5 Common Mistakes Small Businesses Make When Budgeting and Planning Their Finances

Budgeting and financial planning are essential to the success of any small business. However, many entrepreneurs make mistakes that can jeopardize their financial stability and growth potential.

- ✓ One common mistake is underestimating expenses. When starting a business, it's important to account for all costs, including rent, utilities, inventory, marketing, and employee salaries. Failing to do so can lead to cash flow problems later on.
- ✓ Another mistake is not regularly reviewing and adjusting your budget. A budget should be a living document that evolves as your business grows or encounters new challenges. By reviewing your budget regularly, you can identify areas where you need to cut costs or allocate additional resources.
- ✓ A lack of contingency planning is another pitfall small businesses often fall into. Unexpected events like equipment breakdowns or economic downturns can disrupt operations and strain budgets. Having an emergency fund or contingency plan can help mitigate the impact of such events.
- ✓ Additionally, some business owners fail to separate personal and business finances. Mixing these can make it difficult to accurately assess profitability and may lead to tax issues.
- ✓ Many small businesses also overlook the value of seeking professional advice when budgeting and financial planning. Working with experts like Protea Financial can provide valuable guidance on managing finances effectively, giving you more time to focus on growing your business.

8.6 Financial PlanningTechniques for Business Growth

Financial planning skills are crucial for achieving business success. By managing your finances carefully, you can ensure your small business has the resources it needs to grow and thrive. Here are some effective financial planning strategies to support your company's growth:

- ✓ **Set Specific Goals:** Clearly define your business objectives and align them with your financial goals. This will help you determine the steps and investments needed to achieve your targets.
- ✓ **Monitor Cash Flow:** Regularly track your cash flow to ensure you have sufficient working capital to cover expenses and capitalize on growth opportunities. Implementing efficient invoicing and payment systems can also improve cash flow management.
- ✓ **Invest Wisely:** Make informed investment decisions by conducting thorough market research, assessing potential risks, and evaluating return on investment (ROI). Think about spreading your investments across different asset classes to mitigate risk.
- ✓ **Control Spending:** Keep a close eye on expenses by regularly reviewing budgets, negotiating contracts with suppliers, and seeking cost-effective alternatives for essential goods or services.
- ✓ **Seek Expert Advice:** Consult with professional advisors such as accountants or financial consultants who specialize in small business needs. Their expertise can be invaluable in optimizing financial strategies for growth.

Remember that each business is unique, so tailor these strategies to your industry and long-term goals to ensure sustainable growth without sacrificing profitability.

8.7 Tips and Tricks for Staying on Budget

Creating a budget for your business is one thing; sticking to it is another. Here are a few suggestions to help you stay focused:

a) **Set Clear Objectives:** Start by setting financial goals and objectives. Whether your aim is to boost revenue, cut costs, or save for future investments, setting clear goals will help you stay focused and motivated.

b) **Create a Realistic Budget:** Develop a budget that aligns with your business goals and accounts for all expenses, including fixed costs like rent and utilities, as well as variable costs like marketing and inventory. Be realistic with your income projections to avoid overspending.

c) **Monitor Cash Flow Regularly:** Keep an eye on your cash flow to ensure you have enough funds to cover your expenses. Regularly track inflows and outflows so you can make adjustments as needed.

d) **Track Expenses:** Implement an efficient expense tracking system to monitor where every dollar is spent. This can help you identify areas where you may be overspending.

e) **Review Your Budget Regularly:** Periodically review your budget to assess its effectiveness in meeting your financial goals. Make adjustments as necessary based on market changes or unforeseen events.

f) **Prioritize Essential Spending:** Differentiate between essential and non-essential spending in your budget. If necessary, cut back on discretionary spending while ensuring that essential expenses are adequately covered.

g) **Stay Disciplined:** Avoid impulsive purchases or unnecessary spending that could derail your budgeting efforts. Stick to your plan, even when faced with tempting opportunities or unexpected challenges.

h) **Collaborate with Your Team:** Involve key team members in the budgeting process so they understand the company's financial goals and are more likely to support cost-saving initiatives.

Staying on budget requires discipline, regular monitoring, flexibility, and adaptation. Don't hesitate to seek professional help from Protea Financial, who can provide expert advice tailored to small businesses.

8.8 The Financial Planning Process

When it comes to long-term business success, preparation is key. A solid financial plan is central to that preparation, outlining a business's short- and long-term financial goals and how it intends to achieve them. Used by decision-makers, potential partners, investors, and lenders alike, a financial plan typically includes sales forecasts, cash flow projections, expected expenses, key financial ratios, and the break-even analysis. When creating a financial plan, a few basic steps should be followed:

a) **Develop a Clear Vision:** The first step is to define your business objectives and what you want to achieve in the short term (1-3 years) and long term (3-5 years). This vision will guide your financial decisions.
b) **Analyse Current Financial Situation:** Conduct a thorough analysis of your current finances, including income, expenses, assets, liabilities, and cash flow. Understanding where you stand financially will help you make informed decisions moving forward.
c) **Set Financial Goals:** Based on your business vision, set specific financial goals that align with both short-term and long-term objectives. For example, increasing revenue by 20% over the next year or reducing operational costs by 15% within six months.
d) **Create a Budget:** Develop a comprehensive budget that outlines anticipated income and expenses. Be realistic in estimating revenue projections while accounting for fixed and variable costs.
e) **Identify Funding Needs:** If additional funding is required to achieve your goals, determine how much capital you need and explore potential sources of financing such as loans or investments.
f) **Implement Financial Strategies:** Once the plan is established, start implementing strategies that align with your goals. For example, if one goal is to increase sales, focus on marketing efforts or expanding product lines.
g) **Monitor Progress:** Regularly review your financial performance against the goals set in your plan. Adjustments may be needed as market conditions change or unforeseen circumstances arise.
h) **Seek Professional Advice:** Consult with financial experts like Protea Financial to help you navigate complex decisions or provide insights into optimizing your finances.

8.9 Budgeting and Financial Planning:

The budgeting and financial planning are vital components of small business success. Developing and implementing a sound financial strategy ensures efficient resource allocation, informed decision-making, and sustainable growth. However, navigating the complexities of financial management can be challenging for business owners. This is where Protea Financial steps in, offering expert guidance to help you stay on track with your budget, manage your finances effectively, and achieve your long-term goals. By partnering with Protea Financial, you'll have the support needed to focus on what you do best – growing your business – while we handle the intricacies of financial planning. Let us help you build a solid financial foundation for your business, so you can thrive in today's competitive landscape.

✓ **A balance sheet** outlines the amount of cash a business holds, its current liabilities, and net earnings, which are reflected as an increase in shareholder equity.

Table No. 8.1: Balance Sheet

Balance Sheet			
Asset = Liabilities plus Shareholder Equity			
Liabilities	**Rs**	**Assets**	**Rs**
Equity share	1,50,000	Cash	1,75,000
Retained earning	4,28,000	Inventory	2,25,000
Accounts payable	17,000	Land and buildings	6,45,000
Long term debt	4,50,000		
	10,45,000		10,45,000

✓ **Cash Flow Projection**: This is a crucial element of the cash flow statement, a vital part of any financial plan. Since businesses rely on cash, the cash flow statement records the inflows and outflows of cash within a specific time frame, indicating the company's liquidity. A cash flow projection details how much cash the business currently has, where it's being spent, the sources of future cash, and a timeline for these activities.

- ✓ **Personnel Plan**: Achieving business goals and maintaining healthy cash flow requires the right team. A personnel plan reviews existing positions, helps decide when to hire new team members, and assesses whether these hires should be full-time, part-time, or on a contract basis. It also analyses compensation, including benefits, and projects these costs against potential business growth to determine if the benefits of hiring justify the expense.
- ✓ **Business Ratios**: Beyond an overall view, decision-makers need to dive into specific areas of the business to assess their performance. Business ratios, like net profit margin, return on equity, accounts payable turnover, assets to sales, working capital, and total debt to total assets, are used to evaluate financial health. These ratios are derived from the P&L statement, balance sheet, and cash flow statement and provide context to financial data, helping in funding requests from banks or investors.
- ✓ **Sales Forecast**: Estimating how much you will sell in a given period is crucial for predicting cash flow and the organization's overall health. A sales forecast should be an ongoing process and consistent with the sales figures in your P&L statement. The level of detail in your forecast will depend on how deeply you want to track sales and the nature of your business.
- ✓ **Cash Flow Projection**: One of the most critical components of your financial plan is your cash flow statement, as your business operates on cash. Understanding the timing and amount of cash inflows and outflows highlights the difference between profit and cash position. The projection should show how much cash you have now, where it's going, its future sources, and a timeline for each activity.
- ✓ **Income Projections**: Businesses can use sales forecasts to estimate their potential income over a set period, typically a year. Income projections are calculated by subtracting anticipated expenses from revenue. Sometimes, these projections are integrated into the P&L statement.

- ✓ **Assets and Liabilities**: A company's assets and liabilities are listed on its balance sheet. Assets, which include both current and long-term assets, represent what the business owns. Current assets can be converted to cash within a year, such as stocks, inventory, and accounts receivable. Long-term assets, like furniture, fixtures, buildings, machinery, and vehicles, are intended for extended use. Liabilities, or what the business owes, are also divided into current and long-term categories, including payroll, taxes payable, short-term loans, and long-term debts like shareholder loans or bank debt maturing after more than a year.
- ✓ **Break-even Analysis**: The break-even point is the amount a business needs to sell to cover all its fixed and variable expenses, including the cost of goods sold (COGS), salaries, and rent. Revenue that exceeds expenses results in profit. Break-even analysis helps guide revenue and sales volume goals by first calculating the contribution margin, the remaining sales revenue after variable costs that can cover fixed costs. Businesses use break-even analysis to assess expenses and determine the necessary mark-up on goods and services to achieve profitability.

8.10 Four Steps to Develop a Financial Plan for Your Small Business:

- ✓ **Create a Strategic Plan**: Before examining numbers, focus on what the company aims to achieve and the resources required to reach those goals. Consider equipment purchases, staffing needs, and how goals will impact cash flow. List existing expenses and assets to inform subsequent financial planning steps.
- ✓ **Create Financial Projections**: These projections should be based on expected expenses and sales forecasts, estimating the costs required to reach business goals under various scenarios. Accountants may review the plan with stakeholders and suggest how to present it to investors and lenders.
- ✓ **Plan for Contingencies**: Financial plans should prepare for worst-case scenarios, like cash shortages or unexpected

downturns, using data from cash flow statements and balance sheets. Common contingencies include maintaining cash reserves or securing a line of credit for tough times, or planning to liquidate assets to break even.

- ✓ **Monitor and Compare Goals**: Throughout the year, analyse actual results against projections in the cash flow statement, income projections, and business ratios. Regular reviews help spot potential issues early and allow for course corrections.

8.11 Chapter Summary

A well-crafted financial plan gives small businesses confidence in their short- and long-term endeavors by optimizing resource allocation and investment. The planning process encourages businesses to consider how different decisions might affect revenue and when to tap into reserves. It's also a valuable tool for monitoring performance, managing cash flow, and tracking financial metrics. A financial plan not only shows where the business stands but also reveals over time whether its investments have been successful. Additionally, when seeking potential partners, investors, or lenders, the plan demonstrates the business's commitment to prudent spending and meeting financial obligations. A solid financial plan is key to preparation and long-term business success, setting forth the company's goals and how it plans to achieve them.

8.12 Multiple Choice Questions

1. What is the primary goal of financial planning in small businesses?
   a) Maximizing employee salaries
   b) Ensuring proper resource allocation
   c) Increasing operational costs
   d) Avoiding business growth
   Answer: b) Ensuring proper resource allocation
2. Which of the following is a key component of a business budget?
   a) Fixed and variable expenses
   b) Personal expenses
   c) Marketing trends

d) Competitor reviews
Answer: a) Fixed and variable expenses

3. Which of the following is NOT part of financial planning?
   a) Setting goals
   b) Allocating resources
   c) Ignoring cash flow
   d) Monitoring progress
   Answer: c) Ignoring cash flow

8.13 Short Type Questions

1. What is the purpose of financial planning in small businesses?
2. What are two methods to track expenses effectively?
3. Name one financial planning technique that supports business growth.

8.14 Essay Type Questions

1. Analyse how effective financial planning can help small businesses manage uncertainties.
2. Evaluate the importance of contingency planning in small business financial management.
3. Compare and contrast budgeting and financial planning, highlighting their unique contributions to small business success.

8.15 Mini- Case Study

A small tech start-up faces challenges in obtaining financing for its product development. The case discusses the entrepreneur's strategy for financial planning, including determining start-up costs, break-even analysis, and exploring different funding sources like loans or angel investors.

Question:

- How did the tech start-up plan its finances, and what were the key considerations in securing funding?
- What financial projections should the entrepreneur consider when preparing for future growth?
- How did the entrepreneur assess the potential risks involved in financing the product development?

8.16 References

1. Bragg, S. M. (2018). *Business Ratios and Formulas: A Comprehensive Guide*. Wiley.
2. Brown, R. B. (2021). *Entrepreneurship: A Small Business Approach* (5th ed.). McGraw-Hill Education.
3. Zimmerman, J. (2020). *Accounting for Small Business Owners* (2nd ed.). Apress.
4. Stutely, R. (2012). *The Definitive Business Plan: The Fast-Track to Intelligent Planning for Executives and Entrepreneurs* (3rd ed.). Pearson Education.

Chapter - 9: Start-Up Cost Analysis

9.1 Introduction

Make sure you have adequate funds to successfully launch your business by using our guide to calculate start-up costs. One of the most frequent causes of start-up failure is running out of money. Therefore, developing a solid business plan and accurately calculating your business start-up costs is a crucial first step in starting a company. Having a realistic understanding of your start-up costs is essential as it allows you to manage cash flow effectively and minimizes the risk of depleting resources before your business takes off. Additionally, if you plan to apply for a business loan, securing the appropriate amount shows sound financial planning and prevents the need to request additional funds if resources become tight. Understanding business start-up costs can be confusing, as people often use three key terms interchangeably: start-up costs, start-up assets, and start-up financing. Each term has a different meaning, but all are essential for creating a robust business plan and securing the necessary investment to make your business profitable.

9.2 What are Start-up Costs?

Start-up costs encompass all non-recurring expenses involved in establishing your business, excluding assets. These costs, often referred to as sunk costs, are expenditures that cannot be recovered, regardless of your business's success or failure - they are "sunk" into the venture. Start-up costs include expenses incurred to prepare your business for selling to customers. Examples of start-up costs: Typical examples of start-up costs include:

- **Accountant and legal fees:** Any money spent on professional services, such as hiring an accountant to assist with your business plan or paying solicitor fees for activities like registering your business as a limited company.
- **Business registration:** Fees associated with registering your business with Companies House, which costs £12 online and £40 by post, along with other fees such as paying for a registered office address, postal scanning, business incorporation, and setting up certain bank accounts and online services like bookkeeping.
- **Pre-launch costs:** Expenditures on essential materials and services such as logo design, website creation and hosting, signage, marketing materials, menus, posters, renting premises, and any initial recruitment fees needed to hire staff before your business opens.

9.3 What are Start-up Assets?

Depending on your business type, you may need to purchase equipment, machinery, vehicles, and inventory—collectively known as assets. Assets differ from expenses because they appear on your balance sheet as asset values and are accounted for differently. Asset costs and accounting can be complex, but generally, an asset is a purchase that retains some value: if resold, the business could recover some money. This value decreases over time as the asset is used by the business, a process known as depreciation. This applies to any capital expenditure up to £1,000,000 in a 12-month period, known as the Annual Investment Allowance (AIA). For new businesses, HMRC provides an extra allowance in the first year of trading to cover additional expenses such as energy-saving equipment and certain low-emission vehicles. It's important to note that you can't claim the full amount on equipment used for personal purposes. For instance, if you buy a laptop for £500 and use it half the time for personal use, only £250 can be accounted for as the business asset offset against profits.

Examples of start-up assets: It's advisable to maintain an asset register that details the assets you've purchased, along with receipts, so you can claim these as capital allowances on your annual tax return. Common examples of start-up assets include:

- **Equipment:** Referred to as "plant and machinery" on an HMRC annual tax return, this includes equipment like laptops, cameras, computers, printers, office furniture, and cars. It's important to note that cars do not fall under the Annual Investment Allowance, except for certain low-emission models.
- **Inventory:** If you hold inventory or stock, including raw materials such as textiles or wood, it should be listed as an asset due to its resale value.
- **Cash and operating liquidity:** Any funding invested in your startup, aside from loans or other debts, is generally considered an asset and must be accounted for.

9.4 What is Start-up Financing?

The third component of start-up costs you need to calculate is start-up financing—how much money your business needs to operate until it reaches the break-even point and starts generating a profit. Start-up financing should cover initial start-up costs, the cost of acquiring assets, and any ongoing fixed and variable costs incurred once the business is operational, such as salaries, utilities, and ongoing marketing activities. It should also account for any interest payable on loans. How to calculate start-up costs Calculating start-up costs involves creating a financial forecast for the business, covering all expenses before the business opens and up to the point where it becomes profitable.

- **Start-up assets:** Start by listing all the assets you need to purchase to operate your business, including machinery, computers, vehicles, and inventory. For each item, research the purchase costs by visiting retailer websites or contacting suppliers.
- **Start-up costs:** List all the initial expenses you'll incur while setting up your business, such as registration fees and web hosting. Ensure there are no recurring costs involved.
- **Fixed costs:** List all the fixed costs your business will incur in the first year. Fixed costs are expenses your business must pay regardless of how many products it sells or customers it has. These costs are "fixed" over a specific period, such as a month or a year.
- **Variable costs:** List the costs that fluctuate depending on your business's output or sales revenue, such as materials, production, and marketing expenses. These costs are directly related to the number of products your business sells.

9.5 Here's How to Create a Business Forecast:

- ✓ Begin by developing a spreadsheet that itemizes your start-up costs, including assets and initial expenses, and then sum these up. These are considered your business's sunk costs—representing the total funds required to bring your business to the point of launching.
- ✓ In the same spreadsheet, establish a 12-month projection outlining the expected business activities for each month of your first year. For every month, list the fixed costs your business will face, such as expenses for broadband, electricity, and rent. This will give you a clear picture of the minimum monthly expenditure needed to maintain operations and pay your staff.
- ✓ Afterward, model the variable costs, estimate the number of products sold or customers served, and calculate the pricing and revenue you expect to generate each month. For instance, you might predict selling 10 units in the first month, 20 in the second, and 120 per month by the twelfth. Calculate the revenue from sales for each month, subtract the associated variable costs (like material costs or sales commissions), and then subtract the fixed costs to determine the monthly profit or loss.

- ✓ Determine your business's break-even point by calculating the number of products you need to sell each month to break even. Chart these figures to identify the month when your business is expected to sell enough units to reach the break-even point.
- ✓ At this stage, you can evaluate how many months your business will need to operate before it generates enough monthly revenue to break even. Until then, your business will be operating at a loss. Total the losses incurred in each month leading up to the break-even month, revealing the cumulative loss—or the total funds required—from month one until the break-even point.
- ✓ Finally, add the sunk costs to this cumulative loss to determine the total capital your business will need to start up, launch, and operate before it begins turning a profit.

9.6 Chapter Summary

Creating a detailed business forecast involves a systematic approach to understanding and planning for your business's financial needs. By accurately listing and summing up start-up costs, projecting monthly expenses, and modelling variable costs and revenue, you can estimate the amount of capital required to launch and sustain your business until it becomes profitable. Calculating the break-even point and assessing the cumulative losses up to that point further clarify the financial trajectory of your business. Integrating these elements into a comprehensive forecast not only provides a clear picture of your financial requirements but also equips you with the insights needed to navigate the early stages of your business effectively. This thorough financial planning is crucial for managing risks, making informed decisions, and setting a solid foundation for long-term success.

9.7 Multiple Choice Questions

1. What is the purpose of start-up cost analysis?
   a) To calculate ongoing operational expenses
   b) To determine the initial investment required
   c) To analyse employee performance
   d) To predict future revenues
   Answer: b) To determine the initial investment required

2. Start-up costs include which of the following?
   a) Monthly utility bills
   b) Employee salaries for the first year
   c) Initial inventory and equipment purchases
   d) Tax refunds
   Answer: c) Initial inventory and equipment purchases
3. What is the first step in creating a business forecast?
   a) Analysing market trends
   b) Calculating net profit
   c) Allocating resources
   d) Hiring staff
   Answer: a) Analysing market trends

9.8 Short Type Questions

1. What is the primary purpose of start-up cost analysis?
2. Give examples of tangible and intangible start-up assets.
3. Name some common sources of start-up financing.

9.9 Essay Type Questions

1. Assess the effectiveness of qualitative vs. quantitative methods in business forecasting.
2. Propose an innovative financing model for a green energy start-up.
3. Develop a strategy to accurately estimate start-up costs for a new restaurant.

9.10 Mini- Case Study

A mobile food truck business conducts an analysis of its start-up costs. The case explores expenses such as truck purchase, equipment, licenses, and initial marketing, helping the entrepreneur understand how to allocate resources efficiently for a successful launch.

Question:

- What were the key start-up costs for the mobile food truck business?
- How did the entrepreneur prioritize spending to ensure a smooth launch?
- What financial strategies did the entrepreneur use to minimize initial financial burdens?

9.11 References

1. Barringer, B. R., & Ireland, R. D. (2020). *Entrepreneurship: Successfully launching new ventures* (6th ed.). Pearson.
2. Blank, S. (2020). *The startup owner's manual: The step-by-step guide for building a great company*. Wiley.
3. Pinson, L. (2021). *Anatomy of a business plan: A step-by-step guide to building a business and securing your company's future*. Outskirts Press.

Chapter - 10: Funding Opportunities of Small Business

10.1 Introduction

'Funding' encompasses the capital needed to initiate and operate a business. This financial investment supports various aspects such as product development, manufacturing, expansion, sales and marketing, office spaces, and inventory management. While some start-ups opt to self-fund to avoid debt and equity dilution, most seek external funding as they scale their operations. For entrepreneurs looking to understand the necessity of funding, the different types available, and the process of securing it, this guide will provide answers to these critical questions.

10.2 Why is Funding Needed?

A start-up may require funding for several reasons, including but not limited to:

1. Creating prototypes, developing products, and building websites or apps
2. Hiring and expanding the team
3. Securing legal and consulting services
4. Procuring raw materials and equipment
5. Obtaining licenses and certifications
6. Ensuring sufficient working capital
7. Investing in marketing and sales efforts

8. Acquiring office space and covering administrative expenses

As an entrepreneur, it's crucial to have a clear understanding of why you need funding and to prepare a detailed financial and business plan before seeking investment.

Table No. 10.1: Types of Funding

Characteristics of Investment	Equity Financing	Debt Financing	Grants
Nature	No repayment of invested funds is required.	Funds must be repaid within a specified timeframe, with interest.	There is no repayment of invested funds is required.
Risk	Higher risk for investors since there is no guarantee on their investment.	Lower risk for investors as they usually have collateral securing their investment.	No risk factor for start-ups, as no collateral is involved.
Pressure for Repayment	Less pressure on start-ups to adhere to a repayment schedule, but investors may push for growth targets.	Greater pressure on start-ups to meet repayment deadlines and generate cash flow for interest payments.	No repayment pressure since grants are provided for specific purposes.
Return to Investor	Investors seek capital growth.	Investors receive interest payments.	No financial return expected.
Involvement in Decisions	Investors often participate in the decision-making process.	Minimal involvement in decision-making.	No direct involvement in decision-making.
Sources	Angel investors, self-financing, family and friends, venture capitalists, crowdfunding, incubators/accelerators.	Banks, non-banking financial institutions, government loan schemes (e.g., CGTMSE, Mudra Loan, Standup India).	Central government, state governments, corporate challenges, grant programs of private entities.

10.3 Stages of Start-Up and Funding Sources

Start-ups have access to various funding sources, but it's important to align the type of funding with the start-up's operational stage. Keep in mind that securing funds from external sources can be a lengthy process, often taking more than six months to finalize.

Figure – 10.1: Funding Sources in different Stages of Start-up

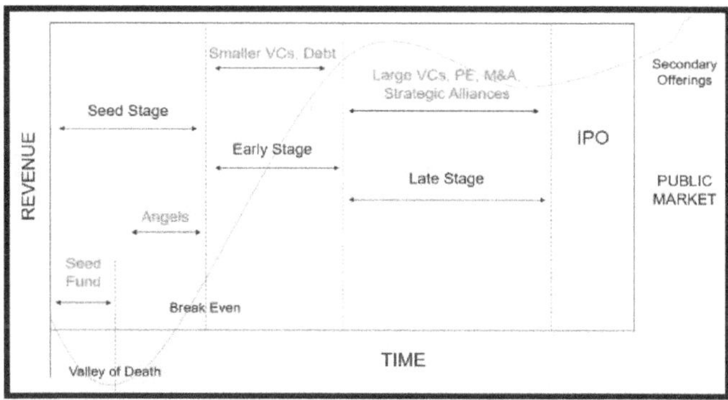

Start-ups can access various funding sources, but it's crucial to match the funding type with the start-ups stage of development. Keep in mind that raising funds from external sources is often a time-consuming process, sometimes taking over six months to finalize.

1. **Ideation/Pre-Seed Stage**: At this initial stage, where you, as the entrepreneur, are working to bring your idea to life, the funding needs are generally modest. Funding options are typically limited and informal. Common sources include:
    - **Bootstrapping/Self-Financing**: Relying on personal savings and revenue to fund the business, avoiding external investment and maintaining full control.
    - **Friends and Family**: Leveraging personal connections for funding, benefiting from an inherent level of trust.
    - **Business Plan/Pitching Events**: Competing in events that offer prize money, grants, or other financial benefits for well-developed business plans.

2. **Validation/Seed Stage**: At this stage, with a prototype ready, the focus is on validating demand and preparing for a market launch. Funding needs increase as you conduct field trials, on-board mentors, and build a formal team. Common sources include:
    - **Incubators**: Organizations that support start-ups with services like office space and legal assistance, and may provide grants, debt, or equity investments.
    - **Government Loan Schemes**: Collateral-free loans from schemes like CGTMSE, MUDRA, and Stand-up India.

   - **Angel Investors**: Individuals who invest in high-potential start-ups in exchange for equity, often through networks like Indian Angel Network and Mumbai Angels.
   - **Crowdfunding**: Collecting small contributions from many individuals through online platforms.
3. **Early Traction/Series A Stage**: With products or services in the market, this stage focuses on scaling operations, growing the user base, and expanding geographically. Funding sources include:
   - **Venture Capital Funds**: Professional investment funds focused on high-growth start-ups, providing significant capital in exchange for equity and mentorship.
   - **Banks/NBFCs**: Formal debt from banks and non-banking financial companies, particularly for working capital.
   - **Venture Debt Funds**: Private funds offering debt financing, often alongside angel or VC investments.
   - **TReDS**: Trade Receivables Discounting Systems, facilitating financing for MSMEs through invoice discounting.
4. **Scaling/Series B & above Stage**: At this stage, start-ups experience rapid market growth and increasing revenues. Funding sources include:
   - **Venture Capital Funds**: Larger VC funds investing in late-stage start-ups with significant market traction.
   - **Private Equity/Investment Firms**: Firms providing capital to fast-growing start-ups with a consistent growth record.
   - **Initial Public Offering (IPO)**: Listing on the stock market, suitable for start-ups with a strong profit track record, enhancing credibility and offering exit opportunities for investors.

10.4 How to Raise Equity Funding

Securing equity funding involves several steps:

1. **Assessing Funding Needs**: Determine why you need funding and how much is required, based on a milestone-based plan and financial forecasts.

2. **Assessing Investment Readiness**: Ensure your start-up is ready for investment by demonstrating revenue growth, market position, and a solid business plan.
3. **Preparation of Pitch Deck**: Create a comprehensive presentation outlining your start-ups key aspects.
4. **Investor Targeting**: Research potential investors, their past investments, sector preferences, and engagement levels. Utilize pitching events and direct contacts to reach them.
5. **Due Diligence by Investors**: Investors will thoroughly review your start-ups financials, team credentials, and claims before finalizing any deal. Successful due diligence leads to funding on mutually agreed terms.

10.5 Chapter Summary

Securing loans or funding can be challenging, especially for new ventures with limited credit history. Understanding the various funding methods and their advantages and disadvantages is essential for making informed decisions. While borrowing can lead to debt accumulation, careful selection of funding sources and partners is crucial for the successful growth and sustainability of your business.

10.6 Multiple Choice Questions

1. Equity funding involves giving up a portion of:
   A. Business profits
   B. Personal assets
   C. Business ownership
   D. Tax exemptions
   Answer: C
2. Angel investors usually provide funding in exchange for:
   A. Debt repayment
   B. Equity ownership
   C. Licensing agreements
   D. Monthly interest payments
   Answer: B
3. What is the primary funding source during the ideation stage of a startup?
   A. IPO
   B. Angel investors

C. Self-funding
D. Venture capital
Answer: C

10.7 Short Type Questions

1. Name two differences between angel investors and venture capitalists.
2. What is equity dilution, and why should founders be aware of it?
3. What role does funding play in small business success?

10.8 Essay Type Questions

1. Develop a pitch for raising equity funding for a hypothetical business idea, highlighting its unique selling point and financial projections.
2. Design a plan for utilizing equity funding to scale a small business in a competitive market.
3. What are the key differences between bootstrapping and venture capital as funding sources?

10.9 Mini- Case Study

A craft brewery looks for funding opportunities to scale its operations. The study looks at different funding avenues like venture capital, crowdfunding, government grants, and small business loans, comparing the advantages and disadvantages of each option.

Question:

- What were the pros and cons of the different funding options available to the craft brewery?
- How did the brewery evaluate which funding opportunity best fit its needs and business model?
- What role did crowdfunding play in the brewery's success?

10.10 References

1. Burns, P. (2020). *Entrepreneurship and small business: Start-up, growth, and maturity* (5th ed.). Red Globe Press.
2. Roberts, M. J., & Stevenson, H. H. (2021). *New business ventures and the entrepreneur* (7th ed.). McGraw-Hill Education.
3. Gompers, P., & Sahlman, W. A. (2022). *Entrepreneurial finance: A casebook.* Wiley.

Chapter - 11: Major Ways for Raising the Start-up Funds

11.1 Introduction

Many thinkers, inventors, and entrepreneurs possess business ideas capable of driving social change. These innovative products and services have the potential to address significant societal challenges. For instance, you might develop low-cost tools to enhance education or create a platform to connect marginalized communities with other organizations. The Indian government has launched the Startup India initiative to cultivate and support the Indian startup ecosystem. This initiative offers various advantages, including tax benefits, simplified compliance, and expedited intellectual property rights (IPR) processing. Even if you have a brilliant start-up idea, securing funding is essential to bring it to life. This article explores the different stages and methods of raising funds for a start-up. A start-up is typically a company in its initial operational stage, founded by one or more entrepreneurs to deliver a unique product or service. Before seeking funds for your start-up, ensure that you have completed all necessary groundwork, such as developing a business strategy, execution and growth plans, and understanding your funding requirements.

11.2 Ways to Raise Funds for Your Start-up

1. **Investments from Close Network:** It is often easier to secure funding from family, friends, and a close network who trust you than from investors or banks. These individuals are more likely to invest in your start-up because they believe in your vision. If you plan to borrow money from them, it's wise to seek legal advice. The advantage is that you can repay the money with flexibility. However, borrowing from close connections can strain relationships, so it's crucial to keep your commitments and work diligently to repay the funds.
2. **Government Schemes:** The Indian government has introduced various loan schemes to support start-up enterprises, recognizing the role of start-ups in driving innovation and economic growth. These schemes provide financial, infrastructural, and regulatory support, particularly benefiting women entrepreneurs, educated youth, and individuals from the SC/ST category, and those in rural areas, thereby contributing to India's overall economic development. Some of the notable government schemes include:
    - Smart Farm Challenge by STPI
    - Start-up India Initiative
    - Dairy Entrepreneurship Development Program
    - Pradhan Mantri Mudra Yojana
    - Start-up India Seed Fund
    - Digital India Bhashini
    - ASPIRE
    - Start-up Leadership Program
    - Chunauti
    - Qualcomm Semiconductor Mentorship Program
    - Aatmanirbhar Bharat App Innovation Challenge
    - STPI
    - Samridh Scheme
    - Digital India Genesis
    - Drone Shakti
3. **Venture Capitalists:** Venture capitalists (VCs) are crucial players in the start-up ecosystem, providing funding to early-stage companies with high growth potential. VCs are attracted to start-ups with clear and ambitious long-

term goals, a resilient business model, and a competent team. They invest in start-ups with the expectation of high returns, usually in exchange for equity. Unlike angel investors, VCs often engage in long-term partnerships, aligning their success with the start-ups. However, VCs typically avoid investing in the very early or later stages of a start-up when competition is intense. In essence, VCs provide both capital and strategic guidance to help businesses grow.

4. **Bank Loans:** Indian banks provide conventional loans to start-ups, assessing them based on their creditworthiness and business plans. They provide two forms of funding: term loans and working capital loans. While the process can be lengthy, securing a bank loan offers stability and allows entrepreneurs to retain full ownership of their business. However, obtaining a loan from private or public sector banks can be challenging if you lack a financial history or good credit score.
5. **Start-up Incubators and Accelerators:** Joining an incubator or accelerator program offers start-ups mentorship, resources, and networking opportunities. These programs often exchange equity for support, helping start-ups accelerate their growth. Incubators and accelerators provide communal workspaces and development centres that can kick start a start-up into growth mode. They also offer various value-added services, such as utilities, workspace, and legal assistance. However, entry into these programs can be competitive, and start-ups may find their vision influenced by the program's objectives.
6. **Freelancing:** Entrepreneurs can fund their start-ups by offering freelance services in their area of expertise. This approach provides immediate income and allows for skill development while also generating funds in the early stages of the start-up. However, balancing freelancing with building a start-up can be challenging, and there is a risk of diverting focus from the core business.
7. **Grants & Competitions:** Participating in grants and competitions can provide non-dilutive funding and industry recognition. Winning these opportunities enhances a start-up's credibility and can attract additional investment. However, the competition is often fierce, and

the application process requires time and precision. It's also important to be comfortable with any grant agreements.

8. **Strategic Partnerships:** Collaborating with established companies for mutual benefit can bring funds and resources to start-ups. Strategic partnerships can create new markets and technologies. However, aligning goals and maintaining a balanced partnership can be challenging, requiring careful negotiation and communication.

11.3 Major Ways to Raise Funds for a Start-up Business

A start up is a company, at its initial stage of operations, established by one or more entrepreneurs to produce a unique product or service. Before collecting startup funding, ensure you finish all your groundwork, such as developing business strategy, execution and growth plans, and understanding the funding requirements. Choose one of the following ways to raise a fund for your start-up.

A) **What is Bootstrapping:** Bootstrapping entails starting and growing a business from the ground up without external funding or with only minimal outside capital. This approach to financing a small business relies on the owner's resources, avoiding the need to share equity or take out large loans from banks. Bootstrapped businesses typically depend heavily on internal financing sources, including credit cards, mortgages, and personal loans. For a bootstrapped business to grow successfully, a competent development strategy that accounts for all potential risks is essential. Additionally, available funds must be allocated to the most critical segments of the business model.

Stages of Bootstrapping: A bootstrapped company typically goes through several stages:

✓ **Beginner Stage:** This stage begins with the entrepreneur using saved money or funds borrowed from friends. For example, the founder might continue working their primary job while simultaneously starting the business.

- ✓ **Customer-Funded Stage:** At this stage, the business uses revenue from customers or clients to maintain operations and fund growth.
- ✓ **Credit Stage:** During the credit stage, the entrepreneur focuses on securing funds for specific activities, such as hiring staff or upgrading equipment. This stage may involve taking out loans or seeking venture capital for expansion.

Why Do People Choose Bootstrapping? Bootstrapping is often chosen by first-time entrepreneurs. It allows them to build a company without needing to attract investors. The reasons for choosing bootstrapping as a business model vary, including:

- ✓ Lack of experience in formulating business plans and entrepreneurship
- ✓ Lack of skills in product promotion and supplier relations
- ✓ Lack of knowledge in raising financing
- ✓ Desire to retain full ownership and not share income with investors
- ✓ Preference to avoid the time-consuming process of finding investors

Advantages of Bootstrapping

- ✓ The entrepreneur gains valuable experience while risking only their own money. If the business fails, they won't have to repay loans or other borrowed funds. If successful, the entrepreneur retains full control and can attract investors, taking the business to a new level.
- ✓ The entrepreneur retains the rights to all developments and ideas used in the business.
- ✓ The lack of initial funding forces entrepreneurs to find creative solutions, offering unique market propositions.
- ✓ Independence from investors allows the entrepreneur to make decisions autonomously, enabling them to create something unique and fulfill their vision.
- ✓ Bootstrapping enables the entrepreneur to focus entirely on the key aspects of the business, such as sales and product development, without the stress of securing external funding.

- ✓ Businesses that build a strong financial foundation through bootstrapping are more attractive to future investors.
- ✓ Bootstrapping allows entrepreneurs to deliver real value to their customers through their products or services.

Disadvantages of Bootstrapping

- ✓ Business growth can be challenging if demand exceeds the company's ability to deliver products or services.
- ✓ The entrepreneur assumes all financial risks, rather than sharing them with investors.
- ✓ Limited capital can make it difficult to attract significant investments or fully realize business ideas.
- ✓ Bootstrapping can be stressful, as the entrepreneur must navigate unexpected challenges without external support.

B) **Bootstrapping Strategy**: Here are some proven strategies for entrepreneurs in the early stages of a bootstrapped start-up:

- ✓ Reinvest net profits.
- ✓ Create a detailed business plan to organize efforts and set a clear direction.
- ✓ Ensure that the business idea (product or service) solves a real problem, ensuring a target market.
- ✓ Seek mentorship from successful individuals in the field who can offer valuable advice.
- ✓ Leverage networking opportunities to build connections with people who can support your business, such as journalists, graphic designers, or web developers who might help out of friendship or goodwill.

C) **Angel Investors:** An angel investor is a wealthy individual who provides financial backing to small business ventures in exchange for equity ownership. Unlike venture capital firms that manage investment funds, angel investors use their personal net worth to fund businesses. They tend to be more patient with entrepreneurs compared to venture capitalists and are often willing to offer smaller amounts of money over a more extended period. However, they do expect an eventual exit strategy to realize their profits, typically through a public offering or acquisition.

The Pros and Cons of Angel Investors

Advantages: Angel investors offer funding that doesn't require repayment because, in exchange for the capital, they receive ownership shares. This arrangement is generally reserved for established businesses beyond the start-up phase, which have shown potential for profitability but still need funds to grow or develop products. Since their own money is at stake, angel investors are highly motivated to help the business succeed, often providing mentorship or even direct management assistance.

Disadvantages: One significant drawback is that angel investors usually demand between 10% and 50% of the company in exchange for their funding. This can result in business owners losing control of their company if the angel investors believe the owners are hindering the business's success. It's crucial to carefully consider how much equity you're willing to give away because if the business doesn't perform well, the angel investor may end up with more ownership than you.

Sources of Angel Investing: Given that angel investors are often wealthy individuals, many business owners seek them out for funding. Some common ways to find angel investors include:

- ✓ **Angel List:** An online platform that connects business owners with investors.
- ✓ **Angel Investment Network:** A worldwide online platform with more than 279,000 investors, allowing entrepreneurs to create profiles and showcase their businesses.
- ✓ **LinkedIn:** A professional social network where you can directly contact potential angel investors.
- ✓ **Local Business Groups or Schools:** Local business schools or organizations may help you connect with angel investors.

Before approaching an angel investor, ensure that your business plan is solid. Investors will want to see that your business has the potential to succeed before committing their money.

D) **Short-Term Financing:** If you want to keep your business agile, you might avoid long-term loans because of the burden of debt payments that could last for years or even decades. However, if a lump sum of money could significantly impact your business, a long-term loan isn't your only option. Short-term business loans provide quick access to cash, and you can often be done with repayments within 18 months or less. Before exploring the best options, here's what you should know about short-term financing.

How Does a Short-Term Business Loan Work? Short-term small business loans function similarly to other loans. The lender provides you with a lump sum of money, typically in exchange for business collateral, unless you choose an unsecured loan, which usually comes with a higher interest rate. Like other loans, you must repay the borrowed amount according to the loan's terms. However, the repayment period is brief, usually 18 months or less. Depending on the lender, you may need to make daily or weekly payments. These loans are primarily offered by online lenders who can process applications quickly, sometimes within 24 hours. Once approved, the money can be in your account the same day, but be prepared for higher interest rates as many short-term loans use factor rates instead of traditional interest rates.

Short-Term vs. Long-Term Business Loans: Both types of loans can be used for various business purposes, so make sure to review the loan agreement to understand how you can use the funds.

- ✓ **Long-Term Loans:** These come with longer repayment terms, typically ranging from seven to 25 years. Interest rates are typically lower compared to those of short-term loans.
- ✓ **Short-Term Loans:** You typically make payments weekly or daily, and interest is often expressed as a factor rate, making the overall cost of borrowing higher compared to long-term loans.

Reasons to take out a Short-Term Business Loan: The reasons for considering a short-term loan are often unique to your business, but common scenarios include:

- ✓ **Handling Emergency Expenses:** Short-term loans can provide quick funds for unexpected situations, like a broken piece of equipment or a natural disaster.
- ✓ **Managing Seasonal Cash Flow Dips:** If your business experiences boom seasons followed by lean periods, a short-term loan can help you weather the downturns.
- ✓ **Seizing Business Opportunities:** Whether it's hiring additional staff to service a new client or making a large inventory purchase to secure a discount, short-term loans can provide the liquidity needed for growth opportunities.
- ✓ **Getting Financing with Bad Credit:** Short-term loans often have looser eligibility requirements, making them a viable option for businesses with poor credit.

E) **Crowd Funding:** Crowdfunding is a method of raising funds for projects or businesses through the collective efforts of a large group of people, typically via the internet. Unlike traditional financing, which relies on a small group of investors, crowdfunding allows entrepreneurs to gather contributions from a broad audience, ranging from friends and family to individual investors. These contributions can vary in size depending on the project and the potential return. Crowdfunding enables entrepreneurs to use the internet's reach to finance various endeavours, such as starting a business, developing a new product, supporting a social cause, or helping individuals in need.

Types of Crowdfunding: There are four main types of crowdfunding, each with its own advantages and specific use cases:

1. **Reward-Based Crowdfunding:** Backers contribute funds in exchange for a reward, usually a product or service. This model is often used by start-ups launching new products and needing funds for development or production.

  - **Pros:** No equity is sacrificed, and it allows for market validation and community building.
  - **Cons:** Many platforms operate on an all-or-nothing basis, and fulfilling rewards can be time-consuming and costly.
2. **Equity-Based Crowdfunding:** Backers receive shares of the company in return for their investment, typically used by start-ups with high growth potential.
   - **Pros:** It allows for raising larger amounts of capital and building long-term investor relationships.
   - **Cons:** It involves giving up ownership, regulatory complexity, and increased reporting requirements.
3. **Debt-Based Crowdfunding:** Also known as peer-to-peer lending, backers provide a loan that the start-up agrees to repay with interest.
   - **Pros:** You retain ownership, the process is faster, and repayment is on a fixed schedule.
   - **Cons:** The obligation to repay with interest, potential impact on credit score, and risk if collateral is required.
4. **Donation-Based Crowdfunding:** Commonly used by non-profits or social entrepreneurs, backers donate money to support a cause or project without expecting a financial return.
   - **Pros:** No repayment or equity exchange, and it's effective for social causes.
   - **Cons:** Limited appeal for commercial projects and lack of guaranteed funding.

How to Choose Which Type of Crowdfunding to Use: The right type of crowdfunding depends on your business's nature, goals, and ability to meet each method's demands. Consider the following:

- **Nature of Your Business or Project:** Reward-based crowdfunding suits new products or services, while donation-based crowdfunding fits social causes. Equity-based is ideal for scaling a business, and debt-based is suitable if you can repay the loan.

- **Financial Needs and Objectives:** For larger amounts of capital, equity or debt-based crowdfunding is preferable. For smaller amounts, reward or donation-based crowdfunding may suffice.
- **Market Validation:** If you need to test your product, reward-based crowdfunding provides customer feedback and validation.
- **Ownership and Control:** If maintaining control is crucial, reward, donation, or debt-based crowdfunding is better than equity-based crowdfunding.
- **Ability to Fulfil Obligations:** Consider if you can produce and deliver rewards, repay a loan, or manage shareholders.
- **Legal and Regulatory Considerations:** Equity and debt-based crowdfunding have more complex legal requirements than reward or donation-based crowdfunding.

Alternatives to Crowdfunding" Start-ups have several alternatives to crowdfunding, which can be grouped into debt financing and equity financing:

Benefits of Crowdfunding for Businesses: Crowdfunding offers several key advantages:

- **Access to Capital:** It provides start-ups with access to funds that might be difficult to obtain from traditional sources like banks or venture capitalists.
- **Market Validation:** By presenting your idea to the public, you can gauge interest and determine if there's demand for your product or service, which can serve as proof of concept for other investors.
- **Audience Building:** A crowdfunding campaign can help you create awareness and build an audience. Those who contribute are likely to become your most enthusiastic customers and advocates.
- **Feedback and Insights:** Crowdfunding allows you to receive feedback and suggestions from backers before officially launching your product or service.

- **Less Risk:** Unlike traditional financing, crowdfunding doesn't require you to give up equity or take on debt. Instead, you exchange your product or service for funding.
- **Publicity and Marketing:** A successful crowdfunding campaign can generate significant publicity through social media and traditional media coverage.
- **Partnership and Networking Opportunities:** Crowdfunding campaigns can attract the attention of industry leaders, potential partners, and other funding sources, leading to strategic partnerships and further investments.

F) **Debt Financing:**

1. **Bank Loans:** Traditional loans requiring a solid business plan and collateral.
2. **Lines of Credit:** Flexible access to funds from banks or credit unions.
3. **Microloans:** Smaller loans from non profits or online lenders, often easier to obtain for businesses with little credit history.

G) **Equity Financing:**

1. **Angel Investors:** Wealthy individuals who invest in start-ups for equity and often provide expertise and industry connections.
2. **Venture Capitalists (VCs):** Firms that invest in start-ups with high growth potential, usually requiring an equity stake and some control over the company.
3. **Private Equity Firms:** Firms that invest in established businesses looking to grow or restructure, often taking a significant ownership stake.

These alternatives can complement crowdfunding or serve as a backup plan if your campaign doesn't reach its funding goal.

H) **Other Ways of Financing:** Aside from debt financing and equity financing, here are other common ways that start-ups can fund their operations:

a) **Grants**: Grants from government agencies, foundations, and corporations are essentially "free money" that doesn't need to be paid back. They can be an excellent source of funding, but they are often highly competitive and may require meeting specific conditions or goals.

b) **Self-Financing**: Many entrepreneurs initially fund their businesses out of their own pockets, a practice known as bootstrapping. This might involve using personal savings, credit cards, or even home equity loans. While this approach allows you to retain full control of your business, it also puts your personal financial situation at risk.

c) **Friends and Family**: Entrepreneurs often turn to friends and family for early financial support. While this can be a relatively quick and accessible source of funding, it's essential to treat it as a formal business transaction to avoid misunderstandings or strained relationships down the line.

d) **Business Accelerators and Incubators**: These programs provide start-ups with funding, mentorship, and resources in exchange for a small equity stake. Accelerators usually focus on helping businesses grow quickly over a short period, while incubators typically provide longer-term support.

e) **Strategic Partnerships**: Some start-ups form strategic partnerships with larger, established businesses. In return for funding and resources, the start-up might offer something valuable, such as access to innovative technology, exclusive rights, or entry into new markets.

11.4 Chapter Summary

One of the most important lessons from managing a small business is mastering business budget planning and managing monthly expenses. Budgeting involves creating a plan to allocate the business's money over a specific period. Effective business budget planning helps estimate which expenses can be covered and prioritizes spending that will drive business growth. This approach helps avoid unnecessary expenditures, ultimately saving money. Budgeting can seem like a complex and intimidating task for business owners, but with a well-thought-out budget, you can navigate even uncertain situations. For small businesses, budgeting is particularly crucial because failing to manage finances properly can quickly lead to debt. If a company's desire for growth is matched with a disciplined budget, it can avoid cash flow difficulties and successfully meet its goals.

11.5 Multiple Choice Questions

1. What is the primary goal of raising funds for a start-up?
   a) To avoid taxes
   b) To expand an established business
   c) To finance initial operations
   d) To replace existing employees
   Answer: c) To finance initial operations
2. Which funding method involves giving investors ownership in the company?
   a) Debt financing
   b) Equity financing
   c) Crowdfunding
   d) Bootstrapping
   Answer: b) Equity financing
3. What is the primary advantage of government grants for start-ups?
   a) Quick approval
   b) No need for repayment
   c) High interest rates
   d) Unlimited funding amounts
   Answer: b) No need for repayment

11.6 Short Type Questions

1. How does crowdfunding work, and what platforms are commonly used?
2. How can government grants support small businesses?
3. Why is raising funds crucial for start-ups?

11.7 Essay Type Questions

1. Compare and contrast traditional funding methods with modern alternatives
2. Discuss the risks and rewards associated with bootstrapping a business.

3. Differentiate angel investors from venture capitalists in their approach to funding start-ups

11.8 Mini- Case Study

A group of entrepreneurs aims to raise funds for a new clothing line. The case discusses different methods of raising capital, including bootstrapping, crowdfunding platforms like Kickstarter, and seeking equity investment from angel investors.

Question:

- How did the entrepreneurs raise funds for their clothing line, and what challenges did they encounter?
- Which fundraising methods (bootstrapping, crowdfunding, angel investors) seemed most suitable for the business model?
- How did the entrepreneurs balance equity versus debt financing in their funding strategy?

11.9 References

1. Gompers, P., & Sahlman, W. A. (2022). *Entrepreneurial finance: A casebook*. Wiley.
2. Stengel, G. (2021). *Funding your business without selling your soul: Alternative financing for entrepreneurs*. Career Press.
3. Abrams, R. (2019). *The successful business plan: Secrets and strategies*. Planning Shop.

Chapter -12: Risk Management in Business

12.1 Introduction

"Risk management" is a systematic and disciplined approach that enables organizations to identify, evaluate, analyse, monitor, and mitigate risks that could threaten the achievement of strategic objectives. It is a proactive rather than reactive process, ensuring that potential risks are addressed before they can impact the organization. In essence, risk management involves identifying and assessing threats or uncertainties that might affect the organization and developing strategies to minimize potential harm. This process includes analysing the likelihood and impact of risks and continuously monitoring the effectiveness of the measures taken to manage them. Risk management refers to the process of identifying and controlling threats that could disrupt the operations of a small business. It is a discipline focused on understanding and managing these threats, which can range from physical incidents like fires to digital risks such as data breaches, or more commonplace occurrences like slip-and-fall injuries. The process involves a variety of activities, including risk assessment, protective actions, and securing small business insurance—all aimed at promoting the business's success and ensuring its long-term survival.

12.2 What is Risk?

A risk is any factor that could negatively affect a small business's ability to operate profitably. If not managed properly, severe risks could lead to the closure of the business. Risks generally fall into two categories: pure risks and speculative risks. Pure risks are events that a business cannot control, such as fires, vandalism, or the death of key employees. Speculative risks, on the other hand, refer to the potential for both positive and negative outcomes resulting from management decisions, such as expanding into a new market or launching a new product. When small business owners and their insurance providers discuss risk management, they typically focus on pure risks, while speculative risks are more often considered by the business owner or leadership team. Effective risk management increases the likelihood of achieving long-term growth and success by preparing the business for potential challenges.

12.3 What is Risk Management?

The International Risk Management Institute defines risk management as "the process of identifying and analysing potential loss exposures and implementing measures to reduce the financial impact of those risks". A risk management strategy aims to protect the business from various types of risks—internal, external, strategic, reputational, or operational. By creating a plan to mitigate these risks, organizations can better prepare for the unexpected and minimize additional costs. However, not all risks are negative. According to the Small Business Administration (SBA), risks can also arise from opportunities, such as expansion and growth, which, while exciting, can pose additional risks if not handled properly. The ultimate goal of risk management is to prevent or minimize any negative impacts on the business.

12.4 Why is Risk Management Important?

Risks are an inherent part of daily life, and this constant presence makes it challenging to maintain control over business planning without considering the potential threats involved in any given activity. By empowering a business to identify and mitigate both future and inevitable risks, risk management enables better decision-making in the present and allows for effective responses to risks as they occur. The viability of a business may depend on its ability to effectively manage risks and establish structures to handle whatever challenges arise. Risk management also:

- ✓ Increases the likelihood of business success by helping to prepare for the unexpected.
- ✓ Saves time and guides decision-making by providing a framework for determining which business opportunities to pursue and which to avoid.
- ✓ Enhances business ownership by making owners more adept at managing risks.

12.5 What is Business Risk?

Business risk refers to any threat, whether internal or external, that can result in a loss of profits or even lead to bankruptcy. Examples include: a) External factors like inflation or financial risks beyond the company's control. b) Internal factors like work culture and management practices.

12.6 Six Common Types of Business Risks

Businesses face various threats that can impact their ability to achieve financial goals, generally categorized into six types:

1. **Financial Risk**: This risk specifically pertains to cash flow issues. For example, relying too heavily on a single customer for revenue or incurring excessive debt can jeopardize a business's liquidity. Key types of financial risks include:
   - **Liquidity Risks**: The inability to quickly convert assets to cash to meet short-term needs.
   - **Credit and Default Risks**: These occur when a company extends too much credit to customers, takes on excessive debt, or struggles to repay loans or recoup loans to customers.

   Financial Risk Management: Businesses can manage financial risks through several strategies:

   a) **Risk Avoidance**: Avoiding high-risk operations or ideas that could endanger the business if things go wrong.

   b) **Risk Transfer**: Shifting financial responsibility for losses or damages to another entity, such as through insurance.

   c) **Risk Spreading**: Dividing assets and duplicating records across different locations and people to ensure that one incident, like a fire, doesn't cripple the business.
2. **Strategic Risk**: These are risks a company voluntarily assumes to achieve greater returns, such as entering a new market or launching a new product. Having a risk management plan helps businesses decide whether these opportunities are worth pursuing.

   Strategic Risk Management: Key steps include:

   a) Identifying strategic risks linked to business goals.

   b) Assessing the risks to determine which are worth taking.

   c) Creating a contingency plan for managing risks that don't pay off.

   d) Establishing guardrails to guide future strategic decisions.
3. **Reputational Risk**: This risk involves the potential damage to a company's image, which can lead to loss of customers, brand loyalty, and employee morale. Reputational risks can stem from direct actions, employee behavior, or associated businesses.

   Reputational Risk Management: Strategies include:

   a) Monitoring the company's online reputation.

b) Addressing issues transparently and quickly.

c) Committing to excellent customer service and employee training.

d) Tracking reputation over time and identifying factors that influence it.

4. **Hazard Risk**: This includes common physical threats like property damage, legal liabilities, and workplace accidents. Hazard risks can arise from unsafe working conditions, natural disasters, or other environmental factors.

   Hazard Risk Management: Businesses can mitigate these risks by conducting regular safety audits, supporting employee mental health, and addressing potential hazards in the workplace.

5. **Operational Risk**: These risks affect the internal operations of a business, such as technology failures, human error, or lack of cash control.

   Operational Risk Management: Effective strategies include:

   a) Developing a framework for analysing data and identifying risks.
   b) Assessing the likelihood and impact of risks.
   c) Training employees to reduce human errors.
   d) Preparing contingency plans for operational disruptions.

6. **Cybersecurity Risk**: As businesses become more digital, the risk of data breaches and hacking increases, making cybersecurity a critical concern.

   Cybersecurity Risk Management: Key actions include:

   a) Investing in fraud protection tools and security software.
   b) Educating employees about identifying and avoiding cyber threats.
   c) Considering cyber insurance to mitigate potential financial losses.

   By understanding and implementing these risk management strategies, businesses can better protect themselves against potential threats and position themselves for long-term success.

12.7 How to Identify Business Risks

Operating a business inherently involves various types of risks. Some of these risks have the potential to devastate a business, while others may cause significant damage that can be both costly and time-consuming to repair. However, despite these inherent risks, CEOs and risk management officers can take proactive steps to anticipate and prepare for them, regardless of the business's size.

- ✓ **Identify the Risk**: Begin by assembling your team to brainstorm potential risks, ranging from customer-related issues to equipment failures. The SBA recommends investing in a comprehensive business plan to help you "examine anything that could halt, slow, or affect the profitability of your business." Once these risks are identified, categorize them by the severity of the threat they may pose to your business's growth.
- ✓ **Analyse the Risk**: Next, evaluate the impact each identified risk could have on business operations, continuity, and future growth. Consider using a SWOT (Strengths, Weaknesses, Opportunities, and Threats) analysis with your team to uncover internal strengths and weaknesses, as well as external opportunities and threats. Afterward, assess the likelihood and potential consequences of each risk on your list, ranking them as low, moderate, or high priority to determine which risks should be addressed first.
- ✓ **Evaluate Risk Management Options**: Starting with the highest-ranked risks, decide how you will respond—whether by avoiding, mitigating, or transferring them. For instance, a customer-facing business cannot entirely avoid the risk of customers entering the premises, but it can mitigate the risk by choosing appropriate flooring to prevent slip-and-fall incidents. Similarly, a restaurant offering delivery services could reduce driving-related risks by partnering with a food delivery service. For some risks, transferring liability to an insurance company might be the best option.
- ✓ **Select How to Manage Risk**: Once you have chosen your approach, it's time to put your plan into action. Using the previous example of preventing customer slips and falls, your implementation plan might involve contacting a flooring contractor at a specific time to select the flooring and schedule the installation. Additionally, you would post clear signage to ensure customers avoid the installation area to maintain safety.

- ✓ **Monitor and Review the Risk**: Establish regular check-in dates to assess how effectively your plan is working and make any necessary adjustments. For example, if the food delivery service you selected isn't performing as expected, you might need to explore other services to better manage road-related risks. It's crucial not to stop at the identification stage. Lay out your next steps with accountability to ensure that each threat is addressed and continue to monitor and review the risk management process.

12.8 Chapter Summary

Insurance plays a critical role in managing risks, with many risks being insurable. For any business occupying a physical space, whether owned or rented, fire insurance is essential and should be a top priority. For example, product liability insurance is not necessary for a service-oriented business but is crucial for businesses where employees handle money or perform accounting duties, due to the risk of fraud or embezzlement. In such cases, specialized insurance companies can underwrite a cash bond to provide financial coverage in the event of such occurrences. When insuring against potential risks, it's important not to assume a best-case scenario. Even long-serving, exemplary employees can make mistakes, so insurance against employee error might be necessary. The extent of injury coverage will depend on the nature of your business; a heavy manufacturing plant, for instance, will require more extensive employee coverage, and product liability insurance will also be necessary in this context. Businesses heavily reliant on computerized data, such as customer lists and accounting records, must have exterior backups and insurance coverage. Hiring a risk management consultant could be a prudent step in preventing and managing risks. The best risk insurance is prevention, which can be achieved through employee training, background checks, safety inspections, and regular maintenance of equipment and physical premises. Assigning a single, accountable staff member with managerial authority to handle risk management responsibilities is advisable. Additionally, forming a risk management committee, with members assigned specific tasks and required to report to the risk manager, can enhance this process.

The risk manager and committee should develop and regularly implement plans for emergency situations such as fires, explosions, or hazardous material accidents. Employees must be informed of what to do and where to exit the building or office space in an emergency. A plan for regular safety inspections of the physical premises and equipment, including necessary personnel training and education, should be developed and implemented. Additionally, a periodic, stringent review of all potential risks should be conducted, with any problems immediately addressed. Insurance coverage should also be periodically reviewed and adjusted as needed. While business risks are plentiful and their consequences can be severe, there are strategies and tools available to guard against them, prevent them, and minimize their impact if they do occur. In conclusion, hiring a risk management consultant may be a valuable investment in the prevention and management of risks.

12.9 Multiple Choice Questions

1. What is the first step in identifying business risks?
   A. Conducting a SWOT analysis
   B. Creating a risk response plan
   C. Ignoring minor risks
   D. Outsourcing all risk management
   Answer: A
2. What type of business risk is associated with changes in market conditions or competition?
   A. Compliance risk
   B. Strategic risk
   C. Reputational risk
   D. Financial risk
   Answer: B
3. What are the two key elements of risk?
   A. Opportunity and profitability
   B. Uncertainty and potential impact
   C. Planning and forecasting
   D. Growth and competition
   Answer: B

4. What is the primary purpose of risk management in business?
   A. To eliminate all risks
   B. To reduce uncertainty and manage potential threats
   C. To avoid taking any business opportunities
   D. To focus only on financial risks
   Answer: B

12.10 Short Type Questions

1. How can a SWOT analysis help in identifying business risks?
2. Why is reputational risk significant for modern businesses?
3. What are the different types of risks businesses face?

12.11 Essay Type Questions

1. Evaluate the role of technology in modern risk management strategies.
2. Discuss the importance of a proactive vs. reactive approach to risk management.
3. Differentiate business risk from general risk in detail.

12.12 Mini- Case Study

A small landscaping business is impacted by unexpected weather conditions and unforeseen client cancellations. The case studies how the entrepreneur uses risk management techniques like diversifying service offerings, creating a rainy day fund, and insuring equipment to manage business risks.

Question:

- What types of risk management strategies did the landscaping business use to handle unpredictable weather and cancellations?
- How did the business diversify its services to reduce reliance on one source of income?
- What steps could the landscaping business take to further minimize operational risks?

12.13 References

1. Chapman, R. J. (2022). *Simple tools and techniques for enterprise risk management* (3rd ed.). Wiley.
2. Dorfman, M. S., & Cather, D. A. (2020). *Introduction to risk management and insurance* (11th ed.). Pearson.
3. Crouhy, M., Galai, D., & Mark, R. (2021). *Risk management* (2nd ed.). McGraw-Hill Education.

Chapter - 13: Managing Risk in Small Business

13.1 Introduction

Small businesses are vital to many economies, offering employment and driving innovation. However, they also encounter significant risks that can threaten their survival. A key factor in the success of any small business is the effective management of these risks. By identifying and mitigating potential threats, small businesses can avoid costly mistakes and position themselves for long-term success. Risk professionals are instrumental in helping small businesses navigate these risks, enabling them to achieve their strategic objectives with greater confidence.

13.2 Steps for Risk Management in Small Business Management

The importance of risk management in small businesses cannot be overstated. Advisors can play a crucial role in helping these businesses identify, prioritize, and mitigate risks through the following steps:

a) **Identify Risks**: Small businesses face a variety of risks, including financial, operational, legal, and reputational risks. Risk professionals should collaborate with small business owners to identify these relevant risks and assess their potential impact on the business.
b) **Develop Risk Management Strategies**: After identifying risks, it is essential to develop strategies to mitigate them and minimize their impact. This could involve implementing internal controls, purchasing insurance, and creating contingency plans to address potential disruptions.
c) **Ensure Regulatory Compliance**: Compliance with regulations such as employment laws, tax laws, and industry-specific requirements is crucial for small businesses. Risk professionals must ensure that businesses comprehend and comply with relevant regulations to prevent legal and financial penalties.
d) **Monitor and Review Risks**: Risk management is a continuous process. Risks can evolve over time, so it's important to continuously monitor and review them to ensure that the strategies in place remain relevant and effective.
e) **Embed Risk Management into Business Processes**: Risk management should be integrated into the daily business processes of small businesses. This approach ensures that risk management becomes a fundamental part of decision-making and business planning.

13.3 Checklist for Risk Managers of Small Businesses

Risk managers of small businesses should follow this comprehensive checklist:

- ✓ Identify the various risks facing the business, including financial, operational, legal, and reputational risks.
- ✓ Conduct a thorough risk assessment to understand the likelihood and potential impact of these risks.
- ✓ Develop strategies to mitigate these risks and minimize their impact.
- ✓ Ensure compliance with applicable regulations, such as employment laws, tax laws, and industry-specific regulations.
- ✓ Purchase appropriate insurance coverage for risks that cannot be managed effectively in other ways.
- ✓ Develop contingency plans for potential disruptions to business operations.
- ✓ Establish and maintain internal controls to ensure the accuracy and reliability of financial reporting and other processes.
- ✓ Conduct regular training and education programs for employees to help them understand the risks and their role in managing them.
- ✓ Monitor key performance indicators to identify potential risks and opportunities.
- ✓ Establish clear policies and procedures for managing risks and ensure consistent adherence.
- ✓ Regularly review and update risk management strategies to ensure they remain effective.
- ✓ Implement robust cybersecurity measures to protect the business from cyber threats and data breaches.
- ✓ Develop a crisis management plan to address potential crises and minimize their impact.
- ✓ Conduct due diligence when entering new business relationships to identify and mitigate potential risks.
- ✓ Maintain accurate and up-to-date records of risk management activities and decisions.
- ✓ Integrate risk management into the business planning process and decision-making.
- ✓ Conduct regular audits to ensure the effectiveness of risk management strategies and controls.
- ✓ Communicate effectively with stakeholders about the risks facing the business and the steps being taken to manage them.
- ✓ Seek expert advice when necessary to ensure that risk management strategies are appropriate and effective.

✓ Continuously monitor and review the effectiveness of risk management strategies, making adjustments as needed to ensure ongoing business success.

13.4 Managing Insurable and Uninsurable Risks

Insurable Risk: Business insurance is designed to protect companies against insurable risks, or the likelihood of a loss. However, even the most comprehensive insurance policies do not cover every type of risk.

What is an Insurable Risk? Insurable risks are those that insurance companies will cover, including a wide range of losses such as fire, theft, or lawsuits. By pooling premiums from many policyholders, insurers can pay the claims of the few who suffer losses while providing protection to everyone else in the pool.

Uninsurable Risks: Some risks are not covered by business insurance. These include losses that are impossible to value, too costly, too probable, or too susceptible to manipulation. For example, most errors and omissions insurance (E&O) policies won't cover lawsuits related to unpaid bills or stealing customers or employees. Additionally, any allegation related to criminal acts or intentional wrongdoing is generally uninsurable.

Examples of Insurable and Uninsurable Business Risks: Consequential losses, like losing a client due to a service mistake, are generally uninsurable. Insurance carriers also avoid covering inevitable risks, such as offering property insurance when a wildfire is approaching, or gradual damage from maintenance neglect. For a risk to be insurable, it typically must meet criteria such as being costly enough to justify a premium, well-defined with a clear, measurable value, and not within the policyholder's control.

External Environmental Changes create a Demand for Risk Management: Businesses operate in environments that change frequently, and these changes need to be considered in planning and operations. Managers and executives must examine both internal and external factors that can influence business decisions. External environment factors, which exist outside of a company's internal environment, can present challenges or opportunities. Monitoring these factors is essential for protecting the business against predictable events and mitigating the effects of unexpected changes.

13.5 Types of External Environmental Factors

There are nine key types of external environmental factors that affect businesses:

- ✓ **Technological Factors**: Technological advancements can either benefit companies or create challenges. For example, the rise of mobile GPS apps may reduce demand for standalone GPS devices, but companies can adapt by developing new products.
- ✓ **Economic Factors**: Economic conditions impact all aspects of business, from personnel well-being to revenue. In downturns, companies may need to adjust their processes to maintain profitability.
- ✓ **Political and Legal Factors**: Changes in government policies can significantly affect businesses. Companies must stay informed about legislative changes to remain compliant and competitive.
- ✓ **Demographic Factors**: Understanding the demographics of a target market helps businesses meet customer needs and adapt to changes in the market.
- ✓ **Social Factors**: Social values and trends influence consumer behaviour, and businesses must adapt their products and marketing strategies accordingly.
- ✓ **Competitive Factors**: Monitoring competitors helps businesses identify opportunities for innovation and areas where they can improve to maintain market share.
- ✓ **Global Factors**: For companies operating internationally, understanding global issues and cultural differences is critical for success.
- ✓ **Ethical Factors**: Companies must navigate ethical challenges, such as managing employees' personal activities that may reflect on the business.
- ✓ **Natural Factors**: Environmental concerns are increasingly important to consumers, and businesses can benefit from adopting eco-friendly practices.

13.6 Chapter Summary

Risk management is essential for the success and sustainability of small businesses, especially in today's unpredictable global business environment. Small business owners view risk management as a mindset focused on preserving assets, creating competitive advantages, and developing talent. Integrating risk management practices into a business is crucial for navigating challenges, seizing opportunities, and thriving in a dynamic marketplace. Proactive risk management enables small businesses to not only survive but also to thrive in an ever-changing landscape.

13.7 Multiple Choice Questions

1. What type of external factor is a technological advancement that disrupts the industry?
   a) Economic factor
   b) Social factor
   c) Technological factor
   d) Political factor
   Answer: c) Technological factor
2. What is the first step in the risk management process for small businesses?
   a) Monitor risks
   b) Identify risks
   c) Evaluate risks
   d) Develop a risk mitigation plan
   Answer: b) Identify risks
3. Which of the following is involved in risk evaluation?
   a) Measuring the likelihood and impact of risks
   b) Purchasing insurance for risks
   c) Ignoring low-probability risks
   d) Eliminating all risks
   Answer: a) Measuring the likelihood and impact of risks

13.8 Short Type Questions

1. How does effective risk management contribute to the success of a small business?
2. What items should be included in a risk management checklist for small businesses?

3. Provide examples of insurable risks that small businesses commonly face.

13.9 Essay Type Questions

1. Identify and explain key external environmental factors that can impact small businesses.
2. Evaluate the benefits of using a comprehensive risk management checklist for small business operations.
3. Outline and explain the key steps involved in managing risks in small business operations.

13.10 Mini- Case Study

A small, independent bookstore is concerned about market fluctuations and customer preferences. The case focuses on risk management strategies such as market research, flexible inventory management, and establishing an online presence to diversify income streams.

Question:

a) How did the bookstore manage risks associated with changing customer preferences?
b) What strategies helped the bookstore survive economic downturns or market shifts?
c) How can the bookstore better leverage customer insights to mitigate risk?

13.11 References

1. Crouhy, M., Galai, D., & Mark, R. (2021). *Risk management* (2nd ed.). McGraw-Hill Education.
2. Lam, J. (2022). *Enterprise risk management: From incentives to controls* (3rd ed.). Wiley.
3. Dorfman, M. S., & Cather, D. A. (2020). *Introduction to risk management and insurance* (11th ed.). Pearson.

Chapter - 14 : Business Ethics in Small Business

14.1 Introduction:

Understanding the distinction between right and wrong is fundamental, especially when running a company. A strong moral compass is essential, and business ethics serve as your guide. To navigate the complexities of business, it's crucial to have a comprehensive, 360-degree perspective on your company and its interactions. This is where customer segmentation analysis can be beneficial, as the ethical priorities of one demographic may differ significantly from another. It's also important not to work in isolation; engage with your employees to ensure that the business code of ethics you establish is in harmony with their values. Ultimately, your business ethics should reflect the core values of your organization. However, this doesn't imply that you must compromise your principles or engage in unethical practices. Below, we explore six compelling reasons why ethics are crucial in business and why they are indispensable. But first, let's examine some potential ethical issues you might encounter, some of which may be unexpected.

14.2 What is Business Ethics?

At its core, business ethics refers to a set of rules designed to safeguard both the business and its stakeholders. These ethical guidelines ensure that a company operates in the best interests of all involved parties. In its simplest form, business ethics may be viewed as a set of rules that prevent a business and its employees from engaging in actions that could damage its reputation. Many basic ethical principles applicable to everyday life also apply to business, such as avoiding fraud, treating people fairly, and adhering to the law. For instance, the Hippocratic Oath is a form of business ethics specifically related to the medical profession.

14.3 The Importance of Business Ethics

Business ethics represent shared values between a company, its employees, and its customers. Having a common moral foundation is essential for building trust, and trust is a cornerstone of any successful business. You can display your commitment to business ethics prominently in your office, but what truly matters is how you conduct yourself. That said, a business is composed of individuals who may hold diverse personal values, making it crucial to clearly define and uphold the collective ethical standards that represent your organization.

14.4 Ethical Dilemmas in Business

Unfortunately, businesses sometimes face situations where the distinction between right and wrong is not so clear-cut. Ethical dilemmas in business frequently make headlines. For instance, companies that offer large bonuses to executives while underpaying their staff often face public scrutiny. While such practices may seem necessary for growth from a business standpoint, they can appear unethical to customers. Although small businesses may not encounter the same scale of ethical dilemmas as large corporations, they are not immune to challenges. Some ethical dilemmas that even small businesses might face include:

a) **Creating a Brand Character:** Establishing a distinct voice and theme for your brand is essential for marketing, but taking it too far can alienate or even offend customers. Many brands have made the mistake of misreading their audience. Marketing requires a delicate balance between business objectives and human values.
b) **Corporate Social Responsibility and Your Bottom Line:** Business is about more than just working in an office; it involves considering your broader impact and corporate social responsibility (CSR). For example, if you run a beauty company and have not made efforts to eliminate plastic use, your investors and customers might view this negatively. However, transitioning to eco-friendly practices could significantly impact your bottom line, potentially jeopardizing your employees' future.
c) **Creating a Great Place to Work vs. Offering a Great Rate of Pay:** Start-ups often have a lot of work to manage but limited funding. This can mean that while you may not be able to offer competitive salaries, you can create an exciting workplace where employees feel valued and rewarded in other ways. This scenario can present ethical challenges, as employees may become resentful if they perceive that more resources are being invested in the office environment than in their compensation.

14.5 Developing a Business Code of Ethics for Small Businesses:

When crafting your business ethics, consider the following aspects:

- ✓ The company's vision
- ✓ Your mission statement
- ✓ Expectations for how employees should represent the company
- ✓ Expectations for how employees should interact as colleagues
- ✓ The diversity within your team
- ✓ How you will monitor adherence to your ethics—will you appoint an ethics officer?
- ✓ Your customers

14.6 What Ethical Issues Do You Face?

The range of ethical issues a business might face could be broader than you expect. Beyond major challenges like financial integrity, legal compliance, and honesty in product representation, there are numerous potential gray areas. Small business ethics also cover issues such as ensuring equal opportunities for all, maintaining a respectful workplace, adhering to employment and dismissal regulations, transparency in dealings with employees and clients, and openness about conflicts of interest. For instance:

a) If you're running late on a deadline, would you deliver a substandard product or service, or discuss the difficulties with your client?

b) How would you respond if securing a key contract appeared to require offering some sort of favour?

c) Are you diligent and honest with your invoicing and payments?

A reliable invoice generator tool can be quite helpful here.

14.7 Ethics are a Big Issue

In today's hyper-connected world, ethics are more significant than ever before. It's much easier for anyone with basic internet skills to verify your claims and expose any falsehoods or misconduct. The recent global exposure of corporate wrongdoing—ranging from banking scandals to food safety issues and environmental disasters—serves as a stark reminder. While it's usually the large corporations that face widespread shame, small local businesses can also suffer significant damage to their reputations. Local or national media can easily amplify the impact of any ethical missteps, with potentially severe consequences.

a) **The Snowball Effect**: Making unethical decisions can lead to a cascade of problems. Like positive behavior, unethical behavior often starts small but escalates over time. Research highlighted by Workplace Ethics Advice shows that incentives for minor falsehoods can gradually lead to incentives for major lies, a phenomenon known as the 'slippery slope effect.' Once a decision to cover up or lie about something is made, it can be challenging to backtrack without losing face. This creates a trap for both business owners and employees, necessitating constant vigilance. Even if no conscious decision to act unethically is made, a series of small, hasty judgments can gradually lead a business off course, eventually resulting in significant wrongdoing that may become impossible to conceal.

b) **Customers Expect a Code of Ethics**: Regardless of how you personally view ethics, customers expect to be treated fairly and with respect. Many major companies make this a priority when selecting suppliers, requiring them to adhere to their ethical standards before engaging in business. Even on an individual level, ethics are crucial. A study by 23 red found that 91% of consumers consider brand behavior a significant factor in their purchasing decisions. Alienating such a large portion of your customer base is not an option. Furthermore, ethical behavior can provide a competitive advantage. Research by Ethisphere shows that companies with strong ethical principles also tend to have higher profit margins, reinforcing the findings of the 23 red study. Consumers are increasingly aligning their spending with their principles.

c) **Good Reputations Mean Success**: Ethics must be ingrained from the outset and rigorously maintained across your business. Otherwise, you will find yourself constantly trying to address problems. A carefully cultivated reputation is built on customers' perceptions of your company as being reliable, fair, open, and honest. An insightful article by Cutting Edge PR outlines several benefits of a good reputation, including:

- ✓ Customers choosing your products or services over competitors when all else is equal
- ✓ The ability to charge a premium for your offerings
- ✓ Increased value in the financial marketplace

d) **You could be breaking the Law**: Ethical considerations extend beyond integrity; engaging in practices such as financial misconduct or environmental pollution could result in criminal charges or substantial fines. For small businesses, such outcomes can be catastrophic. Even large corporations like BP and Exxon have suffered enormous financial losses and long-lasting reputational damage due to unethical behavior. The bankruptcy of US energy giant Enron due to its financial scandal demonstrates that no company is too big or too powerful to be brought down by unethical actions.

e) **Unethical Small Business Owners will be exposed:** As mentioned earlier, unethical behavior will eventually be exposed. The longer it takes for the truth to come to light, the more severe the consequences will be. Even if the ethical issues are not on a grand scale, public exposure of wrongdoing can have dire implications for your business.

14.8 Business Ethics – 12 Main Characteristics

Several characteristics define business ethics, some of which include:

- ✓ Business ethics are rooted in social values, reflecting widely accepted norms of good and bad, right and wrong practices.
- ✓ They are based on social customs, traditions, standards, and attributes.
- ✓ Business ethics can determine the ways and means for achieving better and optimal business performance.
- ✓ They provide guidelines and parameters for the most appropriate practices in the business environment.
- ✓ Business ethics focus on the study of human behavior and conduct.
- ✓ They offer a philosophy for establishing standards and norms for interactions and behavior within an organization.
- ✓ Business ethics contribute to creating a code of conduct in business.
- ✓ They are influenced by concepts, thoughts, and standards generated by Indian ethos.
- ✓ Business ethics can be considered both an art and a science.
- ✓ They inspire professionalism's values, standards, and norms for the well-being of customers.
- ✓ Business ethics emphasize a service-oriented approach from the customers' perspective.
- ✓ They highlight the need for customization excellence.
- ✓ Business ethics stress the importance of social responsibility in business.

14.9 Elements of Business Ethics:

Organizations continuously strive to create an ethical atmosphere within their business culture. Developing an ethical organization requires fostering an ethical business climate. Some key elements of business ethics include:

a) **A Formal Code of Conduct:** A code of conduct reflects the organization's values and helps employees understand what is expected of them. The Sarbanes-Oxley Act of 2002 made it mandatory for businesses to have a written ethics code. This code should align with the organization's values and expectations, serving as a reference for ethical behavior.
b) **Ethics Committees:** An ethics committee oversees the application of the company's ethics code and other relevant policies. They play a crucial role in aligning the company's actions with its stated ethical standards.
c) **Ethical Communication:** Effective communication of the company's ethical values and standards is essential. Organizations should disseminate their code of conduct to all employees and train them to apply it in their daily work.
d) **Ethics Training Programs:** Ethics training programs educate employees on the company's ethical standards and how to apply them in various situations. These programs help employees navigate ethical dilemmas and reinforce the importance of maintaining ethical standards.
e) **A System for Reporting Misconduct:** Having a system for reporting unethical behavior encourages employees to speak up when they witness wrongdoing. This system should be confidential and protect whistle blowers from retaliation.
f) **A Commitment to Ethical Leadership:** Ethical leadership is vital for creating an ethical business environment. Leaders must model ethical behavior and demonstrate their commitment to the company's values.
g) **Evaluation and Accountability:** Regular evaluations of the company's ethical practices help identify areas for improvement. Holding individuals accountable for unethical behavior reinforces the importance of maintaining high ethical standards.

14.10 Chapter Summary

The importance of business ethics cannot be overstated. Ethics are essential for building trust, maintaining a good reputation, and ensuring long-term success. Companies that prioritize ethical behavior are more likely to attract and retain customers, foster a positive work environment, and avoid legal issues. Ultimately, business ethics are not just about avoiding wrongdoing; they are about creating a culture of integrity and responsibility that benefits everyone involved.

14.11 Multiple Choice Questions

1. **What is a consequence of unethical business practices?**
   a. Increased brand loyalty
   b. Enhanced employee morale
   c. Legal penalties and loss of trust
   d. Higher market share
   Answer: c
2. **Why is it important to have a code of ethics?**
   a. To increase revenue
   b. To ensure consistent ethical behavior within the organization
   c. To avoid paying taxes
   d. To reduce employee turnover
   Answer: b
3. **What is the primary purpose of business ethics?**
   a. To increase profits
   b. To guide business decisions with moral principles
   c. To promote competition
   d. To reduce operational costs
   Answer: b

14.12 Short Type Questions

1. What are three key characteristics of business ethics?
2. Define Business Ethics
3. How do small businesses benefit from ethical practices?

14.13 Essay Type Questions

1. Reflect on an ethical issue you have witnessed in a small business and propose a solution
2. Discuss the role of consumers in holding small businesses accountable for ethical practices.
3. Identify and discuss three ethical challenges unique to small businesses.

14.14 Mini- Case Study

A family-owned organic farm faces a dilemma over whether to cut corners on organic certification standards to save money. The case discusses the ethical challenges of maintaining business practices that align with the company's mission while staying competitive in the market.

Question:

- How did the organic farm balance ethical standards with the need to remain competitive?
- What ethical considerations should the farm take into account when deciding whether to compromise on certification standards?
- How can the farm communicate its ethical practices to build consumer trust?

14.15 References

1. Crane, A., & Matten, D. (2020). *Business ethics: Managing corporate citizenship and sustainability in the age of globalization* (5th ed.). Oxford University Press.
2. DesJardins, J. R. (2022). *An introduction to business ethics* (6th ed.). McGraw-Hill Education.
3. Ferrell, O. C., Fraedrich, J., & Ferrell, L. (2021). *Business ethics: Ethical decision-making and cases* (13th ed.). Cengage Learning.

Chapter - 15: Ethical Decision Making in Small Business

15.1 Introduction
15.2 Why Is Business Ethics Important?
15.3 Theories of Making Ethical Decisions
15.4 Common Ethical Issues in Business
15.5 Different Aspects of Business Ethics
15.6 Ethical Decision-Making Business Strategy
15.7 Benefits of Ethical Decision-Making in Business
15.8 Steps and Principles of Business Ethics in Small Business
15.9 Corporate Social Responsibility – Why It Matters for Small Businesses
15.10 Chapter Summary
15.11 Multiple choice questions
15.12 Short type questions
15.13 Essay type questions
15.14 Mini- Case Study
15.15 References

15.1 Introduction

Ethical decision-making in business hinges on core values such as respect, responsibility, fairness, and trustworthiness. Adhering to ethical principles enables you to approach business situations with a sense of fairness and consideration for others. It involves evaluating all available options to ensure that your choices are morally sound. By making ethical decisions, you build trust and enhance the integrity of your business. As a business owner, it is your ethical duty to both your employees and customers, which can significantly influence your sales and revenue, as it impacts your overall reputation. The process of making ethical decisions involves carefully considering the various choices at your disposal and how they align with your business goals. For example, is there a more ethical alternative that could contribute to your success? Understanding ethical issues and identifying the best ethical solutions for your business are crucial. Your decisions should reflect your code of ethics and motivate your employees to adopt similar ethical standards in their daily activities. However, making ethical choices can be challenging. You might face situations were working with a new client, who is a competitor of an existing client, offers greater financial rewards. Utilizing ethical reasoning can guide you in navigating such dilemmas and making decisions that uphold your business's ethical standards.

15.2 Why Is Business Ethics Important?

Business ethics are crucial for success in today's business environment for several reasons. A well-defined ethics program establishes a code of conduct that guides employee behavior at all levels, from executives to new hires. When employees consistently make ethical decisions, the company builds a strong reputation for ethical behavior, leading to numerous benefits, including:

- ✓ **Brand Recognition and Growth:** A reputation for ethical conduct enhances brand recognition and fosters growth.
- ✓ **Increased Negotiation Ability:** Ethical companies are better positioned to negotiate favourable terms.
- ✓ **Increased Trust in Products and Services:** Customers have greater confidence in the products and services of ethical companies.
- ✓ **Customer Retention and Growth:** Ethical practices help in retaining existing customers and attracting new ones.

- ✓ **Attracting Talent:** A strong ethical reputation attracts top talent.
- ✓ **Attracting Investors:** Ethical companies are more appealing to investors.

Failing to establish and enforce ethical standards can lead to serious consequences, as evidenced by companies like Enron, Arthur Andersen, Wells Fargo, and Lehman Brothers.

15.3 Theories of Making Ethical Decisions

Several ethical frameworks can guide business decision-making. These theories provide various approaches to handling ethical dilemmas and can influence how a business interacts with its customers, partners, and employees:

- ✓ **Utilitarianism:** This approach emphasizes choosing the action that produces the greatest benefit and least harm. In business, utilitarianism helps determine the solution that minimizes negative impacts on stakeholders. By analysing potential outcomes, including costs and benefits, you can make decisions that are more ethically sound.
- ✓ **Deontological Ethics:** This theory emphasizes the inherent morality of actions rather than their consequences. Deontological ethics uphold principles such as honesty and respect, regardless of the consequences. While this approach ensures consistency, it can sometimes lead to challenges if the outcomes are detrimental to the business.
- ✓ **Virtue Ethics:** Virtue ethics emphasizes acting according to certain virtues and moral character rather than following specific rules or outcomes. This theory highlights the importance of aligning business practices with core values and ideals.

15.4 Common Ethical Issues in Business

Businesses frequently encounter ethical dilemmas. Common issues include:

a) **Conflicts of Interest:** Occur when personal gain is prioritized over organizational duties. For instance, an employee working for a competitor while employed by your company can create legal and ethical complications. Transparent disclosure of potential conflicts is essential to avoid legal repercussions.

b) **Discrimination:** Unethical behavior in hiring and employment practices can harm a business's reputation and ability to attract top talent. Adherence to anti-discrimination laws is crucial to maintaining a fair workplace.

c) **Harassment:** This includes various forms of mistreatment that affect employees' well-being. Laws protect employees from harassment, and organizations must address complaints without retaliation.

d) **Bribery:** Although less common, bribery remains an unethical practice where incentives are used to influence decisions. Such actions can damage a company's reputation and trustworthiness.

e) **Intellectual Property Theft:** Involves unauthorized use of a company's trademarks, patents, or trade secrets. This can result in significant harm and legal issues for businesses.

15.5 Different Aspects of Business Ethics

Different aspects of business ethics include:

a) **Corporate Social Responsibility (CSR):** CSR involves balancing stakeholder needs with the impact on society, the environment, and the community. Ethical practices in CSR can enhance financial performance and societal impact.

b) **Transparency and Trustworthiness:** Companies must ensure transparent reporting of financial performance and decision-making processes. These builds trust with investors and customers.

c) **Technological Practices and Ethics:** As technology becomes integral to business operations, ensuring the ethical use and security of technology and data is crucial.

d) **Fairness:** A fair workplace promotes inclusivity and diversity, ensuring all employees have equal opportunities for growth and success.

15.6 Ethical Decision-Making Business Strategy

To incorporate ethical decision-making into your business strategy:

a) **Assess the Current Ethical Status:** Evaluate your business practices, including product production, employee conduct, and personal behavior. Align your operations with ethical principles, emphasizing social responsibility, transparency, and fairness.

b) **Create an Ethical Code of Conduct:** Develop a manual outlining your values and ethical expectations. Ensure leadership adheres to these standards to set an example for employees.

c) **Implement Ethical Decision-Making Processes:** Establish processes and tools to guide ethical decision-making across the organization.

d) **Monitor and Enforce Ethical Behavior:** Regularly review adherence to ethical practices and provide mechanisms for reporting unethical behavior.

e) **Encourage a Culture of Ethical Behavior:** Promote an ethical culture through leadership, communication, and alignment of values with customer expectations.

15.7 Benefits of Ethical Decision-Making in Business

Adopting ethical decision-making practices offers several advantages:

a) **Improved Reputation and Customer Loyalty:** Ethical businesses attract customers who value ethical practices, leading to enhanced reputation and loyalty.

b) **Enhanced Employee Satisfaction and Retention:** Employees prefer to work for ethical employers, resulting in higher satisfaction and lower turnover.

c) **Increased Productivity and Efficiency:** Ethical practices foster a positive work environment, boosting morale and productivity.

d) **Reduced Legal and Financial Risks:** Ethical decision-making mitigates the risk of legal issues and financial losses associated with unethical practices.

15.8 Steps and Principles of Business Ethics in Small Business

Demonstrating ethics and integrity involves:

a) **Customer Value Strategy:** Focus on delivering value and maintaining trust, avoiding practices that could lead to customer mistrust.

b) **Accounting Practices:** Ensure financial honesty and transparency to maintain accurate financial management.

c) **Truth-in-Selling:** Deliver what is promised in marketing materials to build and maintain customer trust.

d) **Integrity in Management Practices:** Maintain a reputation for resolving issues and fulfilling promises, setting a standard for organizational integrity.

e) **Customer Service Integrity:** Ensure excellent service before and after the sale to enhance customer experience and loyalty.

f) **Personal Integrity:** Leaders should exemplify honesty and high ethical standards, as their behavior sets the tone for the organization.

g) **Product Integrity:** Ensure product quality and customer satisfaction to uphold brand reputation and trust.

15.9 Corporate Social Responsibility – Why It Matters for Small Businesses

Today's businesses must go beyond profit-making to make a meaningful impact. Corporate social responsibility (CSR) reflects a company's commitment to ethical practices that consider social, economic, and environmental impacts. Customers prefer businesses that show care for the wider community, and CSR can differentiate smaller businesses from larger competitors. CSR not only helps build a positive brand image and attract customers but also boosts employee morale and loyalty. By contributing to social causes and practicing sustainable business operations, companies can achieve long-term success while making a positive impact on society.

15.10 Chapter Summary

Integrating ethical practices into business operations is essential for sustainable success. Companies that prioritize ethics build trust, enhance their reputation, and foster positive relationships with customers and employees. By demonstrating a commitment to social responsibility and ethical behavior, businesses can achieve long-term profitability and contribute to the well-being of the wider community.

15.11 Multiple Choice Questions

1. Why is Corporate Social Responsibility (CSR) important for small businesses?
   A) It provides tax exemptions
   B) It helps attract and retain customers who value ethical practices
   C) It allows businesses to ignore regulations
   D) It increases the business's legal liabilities
   Answer: B)
2. Which of the following is a commonly referenced ethical decision-making theory?
   A) Deontology
   B) Populism
   C) Monopoly Theory
   D) Behavioural Economics
   Answer: A)
3. What is the primary goal of ethical decision-making in small businesses?
   A) To increase profits regardless of the consequences
   B) To ensure fairness, transparency, and compliance with ethical standards
   C) To avoid legal issues only
   D) To focus solely on customer satisfaction
   Answer: B)

15.12 Short Type Questions

1. What are some key ethical considerations in marketing practices?
2. What is the significance of ethical considerations in the context of small businesses?
3. What are some key principles of deontological ethics?

15.13 Essay Type Questions

1. Examine the concept of Corporate Social Responsibility (CSR) and its relevance for small businesses.

2. Analyse the different ethical theories and explain how they can be applied to real-world business dilemmas faced by small business owners.
3. Outline the key steps involved in developing an ethical decision-making framework for a small business.

15.14 Mini- Case Study

An entrepreneur must decide whether to offer a discounted rate to a long-time client, even though the business is experiencing financial strain. The case explores ethical decision-making by evaluating the long-term impact on relationships, reputation, and profitability.

Question:

- What factors should the entrepreneur consider when deciding whether to offer a discounted rate to a loyal client?
- How does ethical decision-making impact the long-term sustainability of the business?
- What alternative solutions could the entrepreneur explore to maintain both ethical standards and financial viability?

15.15 References

1. Beauchamp, T. L., & Childress, J. F. (2013). Principles of biomedical ethics (7th ed.). Oxford University Press.
2. De George, R. T. (2016). Business ethics (8th ed.). Pearson.
3. Ferrell, O. C., Fraedrich, J., & Ferrell, L. (2016). Business ethics: Ethical decision making and cases (11th ed.). Cengage Learning.

****

GLOSSARY

Accounting: Accounting is a system for recording, analyzing, verifying, and reporting the results of financial transactions.
Accounts Payable: Accounts payable describes the money a business owes its vendors and suppliers for goods and services the company purchased on credit.
Acquisition: The definition of acquisition in a business context is a circumstance where one company purchases control of another company.
Addendum: An addendum is a written and signed document that changes or makes additions to a previously signed contract or official document.
Affiliate Marketing: Affiliate marketing is a marketing model where an online retailer pays a third-party website a commission each time the website's referrals generate traffic or sales for the retailer.
After-Tax Profit Margin: An after-tax profit margin is the percentage of revenue remaining once operating expenses, interest, income tax, and preferred stock dividends are deducted from a company's total revenue.
Agent: An agent is a person appointed by a business to act on its behalf for a specified purpose.
Agile Working: Agile working is a flexible way of organizing when, where, and how employees and business owners get work done.
All Rights Reserved: Asserts that the creator of a work retains all the copyright privileges associated with it
Alternative Minimum Tax: The alternative minimum tax applies to high-income earners and is meant to limit the tax benefits that some taxpayers use to reduce their regular tax bill.
Amendment: Making certain changes to incorporated business entities like LLCs and corporations requires you to file an amendment to your formation documents with the state.
Angel Investor: An angel investor can help entrepreneurs and start-ups get the funds they need to help their business idea become a reality or their business grow.
Angel Investor: Individual private investors who provide start-up funding for entrepreneurial companies.
Annual Meeting: An annual meeting is the yearly meeting of shareholders, upper management, and directors (or managing members) of a company.
Annual Report: An annual report is a business document filed with the state that gives a short summary of the business's structure.

Anonymous LLC: An anonymous LLC is a limited liability company (LLC) where the name and contact information of the members and managers are private.
Apostille: A special type of government-issued certification for use in another country.
Arbitration: Arbitration is a procedure in which a dispute is submitted, by agreement of the parties, to one or more arbitrators who make a binding decision on the dispute.
Arm's Length Relationship: An arm's length relationship is a relationship where the parties engaged in a transaction act freely, in their own self-interest, and without unduly influencing each other.
Articles of Incorporation: The document filed with a state government agency (usually the Secretary of State) to create a corporation.
Articles of Organization: Articles of Organization is a document you file with the state to form a legal entity called a limited liability company (LLC).
Asset Protection Trust: An asset protection trust is a unique type of trust that protects your assets and your estate from creditors.
Asset: Assets are any item of value, whether tangible or intangible, that provide some current or future benefit to your business.
Asset-Based Financing: Using the assets of a company (accounts receivable, inventory) as collateral for working capital loans.
Audit: An audit takes place when an independent person or group inspects a person's or business's accounts.
Authorized Capital: Authorized capital is the maximum amount of capital that a business can raise by issuing shares.
Automation: Automation is the use of an automatic process to accomplish a task with little to no human intervention.
B corporation definition: The non-profit organization B Lab certifies companies as B Corporations. To gain such certification, a company must meet high performance, accountability, and transparency standards.
B2B: A B2B is a business focused on selling goods and services to other businesses.
B2C: A B2C business sells its products and services to consumers in the general public instead of to other businesses or the government.
B2G: A B2G is a business that sells its products or services to the government.
Bankruptcy: Bankruptcy is a federal court process designed to relieve individuals and businesses from unpaid debt.
Barriers to Entry: Barriers to entry are factors that work to prevent a company from entering a new industry or sector.

Bearer Instrument: A bearer instrument, or bearer bond, is a type of fixed-income security where the issuer keeps no ownership information on record.

Benefits: Benefits in the business world cover many different programs that employers offer employees for their health and well-being.

Better Business Bureau: The Better Business Bureau (BBB) is a national non-profit organization dedicated to giving the public the information they need to evaluate businesses.

Bitcoin: Bitcoin is a form of digital currency that is offered independently from any government or financial institution.

Block-chain: Block-chain is a type of shared database that stores data in blocks that are then linked together.

Blog: Businesses and news outlets have blogs on their websites to discuss issues, advertise services, or report breaking news.

Blue Sky Law: Blue sky laws are state regulations that help protect investors against securities fraud.

Board Chair: A board chair heads the board of directors, which is responsible for either managing or overseeing the management of a corporation.

Board of Directors: A board of directors is a group that oversees and makes important decisions about a corporation's activities.

Bond: Bonds are debt securities that are issued by companies and governments and sold to investors. As with most debt, bonds have maturity dates, at which point the principal amount must be paid back in full.

Bonus: A bonus is a reward an employee receives that's above and beyond what they normally earn.

Bottom Line: The bottom line is a business's profits that are recorded on the bottom line of a net income financial statement.

Bounce Rate: Bounce rate is a term used to state the percentage of website visitors that leave a webpage without taking any action on the page.

Brand Loyalty: Brand loyalty is the tendency of customers to buy a seller's products because they trust the seller.

Brand: A brand is the public perception of your company's or product's attributes and qualities.

Breach of Contract: A breach of contract is when someone doesn't fulfil a promise they made in a legally enforceable contract.

Bridge Loan: A bridge loan is a short-term, high-interest loan meant to finance an immediate purchase or fill a financing gap.

Brochure: A brochure is a tangible advertising tool that gives potential customers information about what your business does.

Budget: A budget is an estimation of revenue and expenses over a specified future period of time and is used by governments, businesses, and individuals.
Business Address: A business address is the physical address you designate as your principal place of business when forming your small business
Business Bank Account: A business bank account is an account that helps an entrepreneur keep business transactions separate from personal ones.
Business Credit Card: Business credit cards are intended for business use only and are a great way to separate your personal and company expenses.
Business Credit Profile: a business credit profile is a document that shows your business's ability to pay its bills, like utilities, rent, or credit cards.
Business Cycle: A business cycle is the natural highs and lows of a business and the broader market.
Business Financing: Business Financing is the money business owners require to start, run or expand a business.
Business Intelligence: Business intelligence is a data- and analytics-driven approach to understanding your business, customers, and bottom line.
Business Liability Insurance: A business liability insurance policy helps cover the cost of bodily injury, property damage, personal injury, and advertising injury claims and lawsuits.
Business Loan: A business loan is money or a line of credit a business or individual gives to another business for its startup or operations.
Business Manager: A business manager is a person within a company who oversees employees, strategizes employee productivity, and implements company policies.
Business Name Checker: A business name checker is a tool that allows you to search businesses registered in your state to see if the name you want to use is taken.
Business Name: A business name is the alias that your legal entity is registered under.
Business Plan: A business plan is defined as a guide that lays out what your business's goals are and how you plan to meet them.
Business Registration Certificate: A business registration certificate is an official document that allows the state to recognize your company as a separate legal entity.
Business Structure: A business structure is how the business is organized and determines who receives the profits, how those profits are

distributed, and which employees or members perform the various jobs associated with the business.

Business Travel: Business travel is a work-related trip that doesn't include daily commutes, holidays, or vacations.

Buyer's Market: A buyer's market identifies a supply and demand effect where an excess supply of a good exists in the market.

Buy-Sell Agreement: A buy-sell agreement is a contract between two or more parties that gives the other parties the right to buy out the other's interest.

Bylaws: Corporate bylaws are the rules established to specify how a corporation is governed and operated.

Call to Action: A call to action is a directive to a business's consumers to take initiative on a certain task.

Capacity to Pay: a subjective determination made by a lender based upon an analysis of the borrower's financial statement and other information.

Capital Assets: Capital assets are tangible or intangible things that a business owns that aren't cash in the bank, but are assets that the business owns to make money.

Capital Expenditure: The outlay of money to accrue or improve capital assets (such as buildings and machinery) which are not bought or sold in the normal course of business.

Capital: Capital is money or assets that a company has on hand to finance its current operations and grow.

Capital: the amount of capital in a business is equal to the total of capital from debt and equity. Lenders prefer low debt-to-asset and debt-to-worth ratios and high current ratios. These indicate financial stability.

Captive Market: Captive markets are usually smaller markets where the buyer faces a limited number of competitive suppliers and has no meaningful choice but to purchase goods from the supplier in that location.

Cash Accounting: Cash accounting is a bookkeeping method where the business records transactions only when it pays or receives money.

Cash Flow: Cash flow is the flow of money going in and out of a business.

Cash on Hand: Cash on hand is the amount of accessible cash a business has after paying all its costs.

Cash: Cash refers to the company's current assets, and includes any assets that can be turned into cash within one year.

Certificate of Amendment: A Certificate of Amendment is a legal document that a business must complete for the purpose of making official changes to the organization's formation documents.

Certificate of Authority: A Certificate of Authority is a certificate from a state that allows a foreign business to operate in that state.
Certificate of Cancellation: A Certificate of Cancellation is a certificate that effectively cancels your business.
Certificate of Good Standing: A Certificate of Good Standing verifies that a business is an actively operating legal commercial entity with the state.
Certificate of Incorporation: A Certificate of Incorporation is an important legal document that will serve as the official registration document for your corporation.
Certified Public Accountant: A certified public accountant is a professional who has met state licensing requirements for CPA designation pertaining to accounting and finance.
Chatbot: A chatbot is a computer program or application that is designed to interact with users, typically over the internet.
Chief Executive Officer: A chief executive officer is the leader of a company or organization whose responsibilities include creating policies, crafting growth strategies, and overseeing the entire staff.
Chief Financial Officer: A chief financial officer (CFO) is a senior executive who manages the financial business and actions of a company.
Chief Human Resources Officer: A Chief Human Resources Officer is responsible for all human relations in a business including hiring, firing, and training.
Chief Investment Officer: A Chief Investment Officer is a senior-level executive who manages a company's investment portfolios.
Chief Marketing Officer: A chief marketing officer (CMO) is a corporate executive responsible for overseeing all the marketing activities of a business.
Chief Operations Officer: The Chief Operations Officer plays the role of vice president to the CEO and oversees all business operations.
Classified Board of Directors: A classified board of directors is a board of directors that's structured so that different board members serve for various lengths of time, based on their classification.
C-Level: C-level, also referred to as the C-Suite, is a term used to describe a group of a corporation's most important senior executives.
Close corporation definition: A close corporation is a shareholder-owned business that doesn't trade or list its stock on the stock exchange.
Collateral: an asset owned by the borrower, but promised to a lender against non-payment of the loan. The amount of collateral varies from lender to lender. The closer the collateral value is to the loan amount, the more comfortable the lender will be that the loan will be repaid.

Competitive Advantage: Competitive advantage is where a business's goods or services are superior to or outperform the competitions.
Compliance: Compliance means that your business conforms to all the applicable state requirements and has met all appropriate deadlines for your business to remain operational and in good standing.
Consideration: Consideration is what each party bargains for and what changes each party's situation due to the contract.
Consolidation: The definition of "consolidation" in business generally refers to combining different departments of a company into one larger unit or combining separate companies into one.
Constituent: A constituent only refers to the merging companies, never a parent company in a merger.
Content Marketing: Content marketing is a way to increase sales by providing customers with relevant and valuable information.
Conversion: Conversion, as it pertains to owning and operating a small business, relates to the conversion of leads into customers.
Copyright: It's simply the right to copy. A person who owns the copyright to a piece of intellectual property is the only person who can copy or give permission to copy it.
Corporate Charter: A corporate charter is the document you file with the state to legally create your business.
Corporate Income Tax: Corporate income tax is a tax paid by corporations on their business income.
Corporate Indicator: A corporate indicator is a word or abbreviation in a company name that reflects its legal status.
Corporate Kit: A Corporate Kit is a binder that organizes all your corporate documents in one place and looks professional during meetings.
Corporate Resolution: A corporate resolution is an agreement between agents or owners of a corporation to take on significant projects, make important decisions, or engage in certain activities.
Corporate Seal: A corporate seal is a unique symbol that represents your company, and signifies that a corporate action is valid.
Corporation definition: A corporation is a legal entity that is separate from its owners. A corporation can be considered a "legal person" under the law, meaning it can possess the rights and responsibilities of an individual.
Creditor: Creditors are people or businesses that allow others to borrow money to be repaid in the future.
Debt Financing: Debt financing is used by many small businesses when they need to raise money for working capital or asset purchases. Here's a

definition of debt financing and the advantages and disadvantages of using it.

Debtor: A debtor is a borrower who is liable to pay a defined sum to a creditor.

Deed of Trust: A deed of trust is a particular type of legal document frequently used in financed real estate transactions.

Depression: A depression is an extended time of economic downturn characterized by widespread unemployment and market declines.

Director: A company director is responsible for the day-to-day operations of a company including the business and financial operations and oversight of other employees.

Dissolution: Dissolution is the official closure of a business entity with the state. You likely need to file documentation with the state to make this official.

Dissolve: To dissolve refers to separating something into its component parts or bringing something to an end.

Distribution: A distribution in business means a disbursement of assets from a fund, account, or individual security to an investor or individual beneficiary.

Diversification: Diversification is an investment strategy that minimizes risk by investing across asset classes and markets.

Dividend: Payments made to shareholders and are a way to share profits with investors.

Domain Name: A domain name is a website's "name." These names can help your business find additional success.

Domestication: Domestication involves moving a legal organization from its state of origin to a new state.

Downsizing: Downsizing occurs when businesses fire a significant amount of employees to reduce costs and improve profits.

E-Commerce: The act of selling goods or services online. If you sell through your own company website, eBay, Amazon, or on any other digital platform, you're engaging in eCommerce.

Employment Agreement: An employment agreement is a formal agreement that spells out the rules of engagement between an employee and an employer.

Entity Type: An entity type is the legal structure of your business.

Entrepreneur: Being an entrepreneur is exciting. It involves creating or offering products and services that the public may have never seen before. However, you'll need a go-getter mentality and lots of grit to be successful (not to mention product research, funding, etc.).

Equity Financing: Equity financing allows a company to raise money by selling shares of the business to investors.

Equity Financing: Raising money by selling interest in a business to a third party. The advantage: unlike a loan, equity financing does not have to be repaid. The disadvantage: the entrepreneur gives up part of the company and usually, part of the control.

Expense: An expense is the cost that a business owner incurs to operate the company.

Factoring: Selling the accounts receivable or invoices at a discount to the factor, who then advances the business approximately 70 to 80 percent of the face value. Once the invoice is paid, the business owner receives the balance of the invoice amount less the factor's discount.

Family Limited Partnerships: A family limited partnership is a business partnership where the partners are family members.

Fictitious Business Name: A fictitious business name is a name, other than the registered name of the business, that the state gives you permission to use when conducting business.

Financial Management: Financial management is the term used to describe how a business tracks, manages, and assesses its overall financial situation.

Financial Projections: Financial projections are a tool business owners use to evaluate their future financial conditions and profits.

Fiscal Year: A fiscal year is a 12-month period that businesses, governments, and other entities use for accounting purposes, financial reporting, and creating and tracking budgets.

Fixed Costs: Fixed costs are the costs that remain the same during a period of time, regardless of production amounts.

Forecasting: Forecasting is the process of predicting or estimating future performance of a business based on historical financial data.

Freelancer: A freelance worker is someone who provides on-demand work to other businesses or individuals.

General corporation definition: A general corporation is a legal entity owned by shareholders, managed by a board of directors, and run by officers.

Good Faith: Good faith describes honesty and fairness in someone's conduct during the course of a contractual relationship.

Guarantor: A guarantor is a person who guarantees something for someone else. In the financial world, the guarantor definition is a person or entity who promises to pay for something on another person's behalf if that person doesn't.

Holding Company: A holding company is a legal entity used for running multiple companies while limiting financial and legal liability.

Human Resources: A business's human resources department helps that business fulfil many of its obligations and manage the relationships between the business and its employees.

Income Tax: Income tax is a tax you pay to the government based on the amount of income you make.

Incorporated Business: An incorporated business is one that the government recognizes as a legal entity separate from its owners.

Incorporation: The formation of a new corporation, which is a legal entity formally recognized by the state it's located in.

Incorporator: An incorporator is an individual responsible for setting up a corporation and registering formal documents with the state where the company will be conducting business.

Incorporators Statement: A written document that sets up the traditional "board of directors" structure within the corporation.

Indemnification: Indemnification is a clause in a contract where one party agrees to compensate another party if something happens to a third party.

Independent Contractor: An independent contractor is a person or business that provides goods or services under a written contract or verbal agreement.

Injunction: An injunction is a court order that commands a person to either do or refrain from doing a specific act.

IPO: An IPO (initial public offering) is when a company first sells shares of its stock to the public.

IRS: Business owners should know what the IRS is and how it works. They will need to be familiar with how their business will be taxed.

Liability: Businesses have many kinds of liabilities. They include long- and short-term debt as well as potential legal liabilities incurred when operating the business.

Limited Liability Company (LLC): An LLC is a legal business entity that provides limited liability protection, meaning that the owners are usually protected from the business's liabilities and debts.

Limited Liability Partnership: A limited liability partnership is a type of business entity structure with at least two partners. A distinguishing characteristic of an LLP is limited personal liability, which can be extremely beneficial in running a business.

Limited Partnership: A limited partnership is made up of at least two people. One is the general partner and this person oversees business operations. The others are known as limited partners and their responsibilities don't involve the business's management.

Limited Personal Liability: Limited personal liability is when someone's liability is limited to a set amount, like how much they invested in their business.

Line of Credit: A line of credit is a loan that operates like a credit card. You have a certain amount to draw from and use only as much as you need.

Lines of Credit: A pre-set credit limit, usually at a bank, that businesses can access as necessary to maintain positive cash flow. When funds become available, the borrowed amount is repaid.

Management: An LLC's or corporation's management is responsible for making day-to-day decisions to run the business.

Manager: A manager is the person in charge of a business's day-to-day operations.

Manager-Managed: Manager-managed is the structure where members elect a manager or a small group of managers to handle the daily operations of the LLC.

Market Correction: A market correction is a dip of more than 10 percent from an asset's highest price.

Member: A member is an individual or entity holding a membership interest in a limited liability company (LLC).

Merger: A merger is when two or more companies merge into one company or combine their assets.

Microloan: a loan guarantee by the U.S. Small Business Administration for up to $35,000.

Model Registered Agents Act: It creates two different types of registered agents, which it refers to as commercial and non-commercial.

Multi-Member LLC: A multi-member LLC is a statutory business structure with limited liability and flexibility.

Name Registration: A name registration is the name you use when registering your business with the state.

Name Reservation: A name reservation means that your business name is saved for your exclusive use for a defined period.

No Par Value Shares: No par value shares are stocks issued without a par value listed on the face of the certificate.

Notice of Litigation: A Notice of Litigation is a legal document that informs the recipient of an impending lawsuit.

Operating Agreement: An operating agreement is a document that clearly outlines an LLC's rules and structure.

Outsourcing: When one company hires another company or person to handle projects.

Par Value: Par value refers to a security's value as stated in a company's corporate charter.

Partner: A partner is an individual who formally agrees to jointly manage and operate a business with someone else.
Partnership Agreement: A partnership agreement is a contract that governs how a small business runs its internal affairs.
Pass-Through Taxation: Pass-through taxation is a tax treatment that allows all income, losses, credits, and deductions of a business to pass through to the owner or owners.
Patent: A patent is a type of intellectual property granted to an inventor to help protect their invention from being made or sold by competitors.
Perpetual Existence: Perpetual existence means that a company can remain a legal entity perpetually regardless of a change in ownership.
Preferred Stock: Preferred stock is considered an equity security and it includes features of both common stocks and bonds.
President: A president is a leader in a company's executive branch.
Private Lender: An institution or individual who provides debt financing
Professional Association: A professional association is an organization that benefits people working in a particular industry.
Professional corporation definition: A professional corporation is a corporation in which only individuals with state licenses to practice the same profession can own shares of the business.
Professional LLC: A professional limited liability company is an LLC with members who are licensed to provide specific professional services.
Promissory Note: A promissory note is a legally binding agreement between a borrower and a lender.
Promoter: A promoter is a person or a business responsible for financing or acquiring financing for a project or investment activity.
Property Tax: Property tax is a tax levied on property that an individual or legal entity owns.
Proxy: In corporate terminology, a proxy is an agent who attends a corporation's shareholder meeting and votes for a shareholder who couldn't attend in person.
Public benefit corporation definition: A public benefit corporation is a for-profit corporation whose purpose is to provide a benefit to society (such as improving the environment or promoting good health) in addition to making a profit for shareholders.
Punitive Damages: Punitive damages are a category of damages a plaintiff can seek against a defendant in a civil lawsuit.
Quorum: A quorum is the minimum number of voting members that need to attend a meeting for the meeting to be effective.
Receiver: A receiver is a person appointed to care for your business when you need help managing your credit, property, assets, or operations.

Recession: A recession is a significant decline in economic activity in a given region that lasts for an extended period of time.
Regulations: Regulations are authoritative rule[s] dealing with details or procedures for businesses.
Reinstated Articles of Incorporation: Restated Articles of Incorporation is a business document that combines a corporation's Articles of Incorporation with any amendments on file.
Reinstatement: Reinstatement is the process of having your business go from being in bad standing to being in good standing with the government.
Resolution: A corporate resolution is a legal document detailing and confirming a formal decision made by the board of directors.
Respondent Superior: A Respondent Superior is a doctrine that holds an employer legally and financially accountable for injuries and property damage caused by its employees while they are working.
Retained Earnings: Retained earnings are a company's earnings that remain in the business after paying shareholder dividends.
Revolving Line of Credit: A fixed line of credit a business can draw upon as necessary. As the funds are used the available credit is decreased. As the loan is repaid, the line is replenished.
Rights of First Refusal: A contract containing a right of first refusal gives the holder the right to purchase an asset or enter into a business contract before anyone else.
Surety Bonds: A surety bond is a bond that a contractor purchases to guarantee that it will complete a contract. If the contractor fails to complete the contracted work, the surety bond is used to pay for completion. Small businesses often have difficulty obtaining surety bonds.
Takeover: A takeover is when one company assumes control of another company.
Tax Elections: Tax elections are selections regarding tax treatment where the taxpayer elects how they want the Internal Revenue Service (IRS) and state taxing agency to tax their income.
Tax Shelter: Tax shelters are legal strategies that can decrease or defer your tax liability. They come in a variety of different forms and methods and can offer significant benefits if used properly.
Tort: A tort is a wrongful act or omission that harms another person, resulting in civil legal liability.
Treasurer: A treasurer is the person in charge of managing and accounting for funds within a business organization.

Underwriter: Underwriters are a part of the business loan and business insurance process. They can help approve applications based on several factors.

Venture Capital: Funds invested in private companies in return for equity in the form of preferred stock, a share in the profits, royalties or capital appreciation of common stock.

Venture Capital: Venture Capital, by definition, is start-up money you receive from an investor in exchange for giving that investor a piece of your business.

Voluntary Dissolution: Voluntary dissolution involves closing your business on your terms with the shareholders' or owners' approval.

Voting Rights: Voting rights are the rights of shareholders to make decisions about the company.

Website: A website is a collection of digital pages on the World Wide Web and accessible through the internet.

What is a C corporation? (C Corp): C Corps are the most popular type of corporation. It taxes its owners (shareholders) separately from the business. All C Corps must have the following governing positions: president or CEO, treasurer, and secretary.

What is an EIN: An EIN is a unique, nine-digit number used to identify a business entity. This identifier is very similar to a Social Security Number (SSN), but for businesses rather than individuals.

Winding Up: Winding up is one step in dissolution, where the owners work to "wind up" the business operations.

Working Capital: Working capital equals your company's assets minus your company's liabilities.

****

www.ingramcontent.com/pod-product-compliance
Ingram Content Group UK Ltd.
Pitfield, Milton Keynes, MK11 3LW, UK
UKHW062311290726
14090UKWH00018B/1003